Through the Lens of Love & Truth

A Look at Christian Conservatism in America

A. Travis

ISBN 978-1-7335626-1-4

Printed in the United States of America

Published by FUSION Publishing Group
Butler, Pennsylvania

Visit https://www.loveandtruthbook.com or email loveandtruthbook@gmail.com

Edited by Mindi Stearns, Printworthy Proofreading
Graphic design by Susan McConville-Harrer,
SMH Illustration & Design
Photo credit for "About" page: Marta Greca, MEDIA—
The Creative Agency

Through the Lens of Love & Truth

A Look at Christian Conservatism in America

Dedication

To my husband, Perry Travis, the kindest, most
generous man I've ever known
and a true Patriot

Worldview

A filter through which we

judge institutions, events, and

individuals. It affects our

outlook, attitude, and

perspective on the world.

Introduction

We live in unprecedented times.

That may well be the understatement of the year. Amidst the uncertainly of tomorrow, our friends and family are wondering what in the world is going on? It may seem like the world as we know it is coming to an end. As the chaos continues to build, believers in Jesus are being asked more difficult questions than ever before. Many of our friends and family are reaching out to us for hope with a longing to establish a sense of normalcy.

America was founded on Judeo-Christian values, but recently alternative views that challenge our core beliefs have been exalted as the new norm. The question that plagues us all— is Christianity even relevant in a post-postmodern culture where facts are considered subjective and opinions are exalted above truth?

Without question, times have changed. Like many of you, I grew up in the era before the internet, before the rise of terrorism, and before global pandemics. Even if you are under the age of thirty, you recognize the world is changing at warp speed and there's no going back.

In the past ten years we've watched as every foundation of our existence here on planet Earth has been uprooted. The American dream of finding a job, getting married, and starting a family isn't as straightforward or acceptable as it once was. Even the basic truths of our identity as male and female are being challenged. For reasons beyond our control, life doesn't seem very simple right now.

From my current vantage point (the summer of 2020) we've witnessed every traditional institution— schools, churches, hospitals, and malls—as well as all social norms, such as attending birthday parties, going to concerts or sporting events, and even shaking hands, are either disrupted or entirely uprooted.

Now more than ever, we as believers in Jesus Christ have the urgent obligation to "Always be prepared to give an answer to everyone who asks you to give the reason for the hope that you have. But do this with gentleness and respect" (1 Peter 3:15 NIV).

The problem IS NOT that the Bible isn't relevant today. It's that we don't know how to apply it in the current secular landscape of 21st century America.

This book is intended to provide answers to your friends, family, and acquaintances who may be struggling to resolve their questions. This book provides tools to help you engage others in discussions about our purpose on earth, and God's involvement in the social and political environment of our world today.

Please recognize that this guide is written to give simple, candid, conversational answers to extremely complex questions. This is NOT written to be a deep, theological discussion of theories and concepts related to doctrine.

My intention is to provide biblically-sound and yet culturally relevant answers to real-world questions. It can be a challenge to answer questions about God and his plan for humanity to our friends and family, particularly when they don't share our same belief system. Often, quoting Scripture or "christianese" terms to answer a confused or hurting friend who doesn't even believe that God exists, may not be the most effective approach.

Please join me as we explore how to apply God's character and nature in new ways within the context of our current culture, without compromising the non-negotiables.

Part I:
Ground-Rules

That's Not How this Works!

I remember the first time I met Jackson. Jackson and about twenty other young adults had recently come from Rwanda and Uganda, East Africa to attend La Roche College near where we lived. On this Sunday morning, he and his friends walked over two miles from their dorms on campus to our church to attend service. Because of the logistical challenges of being in a new country, these students didn't drive and didn't have access to transportation.

My mom was working as a secretary at the church at that time and became very close with this group of students. She worked with a couple of other staff members to make sure that these young people had everything they needed to navigate their new surroundings. She invited them to join us at home for Christmas and other holidays since they were far away from their homes and families. There were a lot of challenges to adjusting to a new country and new culture, and my mom was very instrumental in easing that adjustment.

Mom enlisted my dad to drive this group to church every Sunday so they wouldn't have to walk. He really enjoyed this group and grew close to several of the guys who looked to him as they would a father.

One afternoon on the drive back to the college after church, my dad reminded the group that the next week was daylight savings time. This was a new concept for these young men and women so Dad explained how they will need to move their clocks ahead one hour. If they didn't change their clocks, he warned, they would be late and would miss their ride to church.

After a few minutes of muffled silence, Jackson—the self-appointed leader of the group and Dad's co-pilot for the van rides—declared boldly that the group discussed it and they were not going to *do* daylight savings time. The idea of changing the time didn't make any sense to them and they planned to keep the same schedule they were currently following.

Well, that didn't go over too well with Dad.

Dad wasn't a big guy, but still commanded attention when he spoke. My father—in his own inimitable way—told Jackson in no uncertain terms, "THAT'S NOT HOW THIS WORKS. You will move your clocks ahead one hour, and you will be ready an hour earlier next week when I come to get you."

And they did.

What is a Worldview?

A worldview is a collection of attitudes, values, stories, and expectations about the world around us, which inform our every thought and action.[1] A worldview is a filter through which we judge institutions, events, and individuals. It affects our outlook, attitude, and perspective on the world.

Think of a worldview as a lens on glasses. During the solar eclipse that occurred in August of 2017, the moon orbited between the sun and the earth, partially blocking the sun from reaching the earth. Due to the rare nature of solar eclipses, the anticipation of the event was highly publicized. Those wishing to view the eclipse were encouraged to purchase special glasses with cardboard frames and solar filters. Harmful rays caused by electromagnetic radiation could be produced, experts warned, causing blindless for anyone looking directly into the shadow cast by the moon.

These glasses didn't have a magical quality that changed the properties of the celestial bodies. The sun and moon didn't change; only the way we saw them did.

The quality of the lens you use to view objects is extremely important and directly impacts how you see the object you're viewing. If you have ever had to give up watching the big game on your 65-inch 4K Smart TV in favor of your friend's old 19-inch set sitting on a dresser, you understand this.

In the same way that not all TVs are created equal, neither are worldviews. A poor-quality lens can create blind spots and distort the object being viewed.

This is also true of how we view what's happening in America today. One thing I've noticed in recent days is our tendency to want to view the Bible through the lens of current culture rather than the other way around. The moral, ethical, and rational judgements taught in Scripture which governed the last several centuries have somehow "expired" or have been retired. Rather than looking at culture through the lens of biblical truth, we subscribe to the theory that it doesn't work that way anymore. Even many of us who have attended church all of our lives and read the Bible can fall into that trap.

A 2003 Barna Group study suggested that a "large share of the nation's moral and spiritual challenges is directly attributable to the absence of a biblical worldview among Americans." In the article, the definition of "biblical worldview" used in the research is defined as "believing that absolute moral truths exist; that such truth is defined by the Bible; and firm belief in specific religious views."

The survey concluded that 4% of all adults, and only 9% of those identifying as born-again Christians, rely on this worldview for their decision-making.[2]

In contrast, we live in a society that believes the rules change based on popular opinion. Instead of embracing truth, many have chosen to tell their own story about the facts, regardless of their factual and historical accuracy. We need only to turn on the evening news to see competing opinions describing the same scene. In the last few decades, the idea of narratives has replaced objective truth.

A narrative, according to Merriam-Webster is "a way of presenting or understanding a situation or series of events that reflects and promotes a particular point of view or set of values." Many have allowed feelings and opinions about the facts to be more important than the truth.

Can the truth change simply because we would like it to change?

The Game of Life

I've spent a lot of time over the past few years contemplating this and like to think of it in this way—life is like a game.

I'm an avid sports fan—football, baseball, hockey. I played and coached soccer most of my life. One of the first things that you need to learn in order to be successful in any sport is the rules of the game. If, for example, a wide receiver in the NFL fails to plant both feet inbounds while possessing the ball, the pass is called incomplete. It doesn't matter how sincerely he believes college rules still apply or how adamantly he protests; the ball will not advance.

Rules play an important part in any game. I remember as a kid playing pickup wiffleball with my brothers and the other kids in the neighborhood where my grandmother lived. We would gather in the parking lot across the street from her house when-ever we visited. We spent half our time playing the game and the other half arguing about the rules. I learned an important lesson from that experience—when everyone tries to play the game by their own set of rules, the outcome is certain: nobody wins.

NOBODY WINS! It's worth repeating.

All the type-A personalities like myself understand that if you can't win, there's no reason to play the game. Yes, I was the child who took my ball and went home when I lost.

Who's on First?

This got me thinking...*In the game of life, who makes the rules? Who gets to change the rules?*

In 2018 rules were changed in Major League Base-ball to increase the speed of the game. The MLB added a pitch clock and limited the number of mound vis-its by the pitching coach. Commercial breaks were also shortened.[3] Players, coaches, and even fans peti-tioned for years to speed up the pace of the game, but ultimately the commissioner's office is the only one authorized to make such changes.

Individual players don't get to decide which rules they are going to follow and which they aren't. Only the institution which oversees the league—the MLB—has that authority.

This is true in sports and this is true in life. As a fol-lower of Jesus Christ, I came to the conclusion a long time ago that if I truly believe that God is the author and Creator of the universe, then I need to acknowledge that I don't make the rules.

Think about the rules of the game outlined in the first couple chapters of Genesis: God created the heavens and earth in one day with a spoken word (Genesis 1:1); He created the animal kingdom according to their kinds (1:24); Created male and female in his image and likeness (1:27); He instituted marriage between a man and a woman (2:24); and gave the human race the ability (and obligation) to choose between good and evil (3:22).

> When everyone tries to play the game by their own set of rules, the outcome is certain: nobody wins.

These rules sound easy enough, right? Yet every single one is currently being contested in our society today.

This trend is very troubling. The laws of nature that have governed the previous thousands of years, in every culture in every country on the planet, are suddenly contested. Once upon a time marriage was thought to be exclusively between one man and one woman. Once upon a time babies were born either male or female. Once upon a time murder, assault, and theft were punishable offenses. New narratives about marriage, sexuality, and the new normal leave many of us angry and confused.

The entire Christian worldview can be summed up in this way: His game; His rules. We didn't make the rules and we don't get to change them. The Bible is clear that "Jesus Christ is the same yesterday, today, and forever" (Hebrews 13:8).

In the story at the beginning of this chapter, Jackson and his friends didn't get to decide what time it was. They didn't have the authority. They could have chosen to ignore my dad and not move their clocks ahead an hour, but they would have suffered consequences. They would have been late all the time.

Ahhh...consequences! Remember those?

If the rules haven't changed, why are many in our society convinced that they have? Something has changed, but it's hard to nail down exactly what. My observation is that this culture has done a stellar job of separating choices from consequences. We believe that everyone gets to choose their own truth. Not only can we make our own decisions about right and wrong, but we also get to choose the benefits/consequences of our actions. But is that really the case? It's my personal conviction that it is intellectually dishonest to believe that everyone can be right at the same time. That's not how this works.

Something else is at play here, as well. If I deliberately ignore the connection between my actions and the consequences, I am no longer responsible and I am now the victim. I can't be held accountable for my actions because I am the victim. As the victim, someone else is responsible to fix it—my parents, my spouse, the school system, or the government.

In 2016 the band Brothers Osbourne came out with the song, "It Ain't My Fault."[4] The story is about a young man who goes to a place he knows he shouldn't be, drinks way more than he knows he should, gets in a fight because he says something he shouldn't have said, and ends up in bed with someone he didn't walk in with. But, as he says, it's not his fault.

Many of us in this culture are like the man in the song. It's way too easy to throw up our hands and say it's not my fault that my marriage failed; I can't be responsible for my children's decisions; I can't help living this lifestyle because this is how I was born; I'll never be successful because of the color of my skin.

I do want to stop for a second and recognize that there are times in life when we pay the price for someone else's choices. Children are victimized every day by evil, self-serving adults. Entire masses of people have been denied their basic human rights and freedoms. I would imagine that there are people reading this now who took their marriage vows very seriously and committed themselves to the relationship, only to find that their spouse has been unfaithful and unashamed about it.

Even when we are victims, however, we don't have to remain trapped in someone else's consequences. Responsible people ditch the victim card and take charge of their own life, even when it's painful and hard work.

My friends in law enforcement tell stories of how common (and tragic) the victim-mentality can be. If an officer had a dollar for every time a suspect said, "you're about to ruin my life" or "why are you doing this to me?" he would be at the beach rather than on the beat. The hard truth is that you brought this on yourself. The cop didn't make you shoplift, drive drunk, hit your girlfriend, or anything of the sort. Sadly, some individuals become very proficient at passing the buck on all personal responsibility.

Looking through the lens of the Christian worldview requires that we recognize God's authority as the One who invented the game and makes the rules. Many of the things that happen to us in life—the good, the bad, the ugly—are the direct result of our own actions. We are not innocent, helpless people victimized by an evil society intentionally holding us back. We experience benefits when we obey the rules God set in place to protect and promote us, and we suffer consequences when we reject his design for humanity.

Paul said, "I can do anything I want, but not everything is going to benefit me" (1 Corinthians 10:23).

The same applies today. I can make any choice I want, but not all choices will bring the desired result. When I choose to honor God through being faithful to my spouse, raising my children to respect authority, and making an honest living, I will experience benefits in my relationships and career. Poor choices, however, could imprison me—physically, spiritually, and emotionally.

To return to the game of life analogy...

Why is it that professional athletes are willing to follow the rules of the NFL, MLB, NBA, or any other sport? If you break it down, you realize that players follow the rules because if they don't, they will not only lose the game, but could jeopardize their $20M/year contracts.

Make no mistake, my friends...consequences exist, even when you can't see them or wish to deny their existence.

Galatians 6:7 says this, "Do not be deceived: God cannot be mocked. A man reaps what he sows" (NIV). You can call it reaping what you sow, cause and effect, or Karma. The result is the same.

The reason professional athletes follow the rules of the game is because they have too much to lose if they don't, and SO DO WE. We also have a lot to lose when we don't follow the rules. We don't get to make up the game as we go along. That's not how this works.

DISCUSSION GUIDE

Chapter 1: That's Not How This Works!

The purpose of this section is to help you facilitate a meaningful discussion surrounding the material in this chapter. Please refer to Appendix: Tips for Leading Small Group Discussions.

1. Can you summarize the main idea of this chapter?

1. How does the author complete this sentence, "His game; His _____"? What does that mean?

1. Explain the term "worldview" in your own words.

1. How would you characterize your personal worldview?

1. Have you ever been in a situation where you thought you were the victim, but later had a change of heart and took responsibility for your part? What was the outcome?

1. Can you give a personal example of what Paul meant when he said, "I can do anything I want, but not everything is going to benefit me"?

Verses to read and discuss:

- John 1:1–5

- I Corinthians 10:23–24

- II Timothy 1:7

A video for this chapter can be found on the FUSION Leadership Group site: https://www.fusionleadership.site/introductiontobiblicalworldview

In the Beginning

I saw a program on the History Channel a while back talking about the Tower of Babel, the structure referred to in Genesis 11. The account in Genesis describes how the people of the day came together to build a tower reaching to the heavens. God wasn't pleased when He witnessed what was happening and came down to check it out.

> The Lord said, "If as one people speaking the same language, they have begun to do this, then nothing they plan to do will be impossible for them. Come, let us go down and confuse their language so they will not understand each other" (Genesis 11:6–7).

The show was part of the "Ancient Aliens Series" and it discussed how archeologists discovered the remainder of this amazing and sophisticated tower. This program provided speculation on its origins. It concluded that the only reasonable explanation is that aliens helped human beings build the tower! These aliens came to earth, constructed the tower, and returned to where they came from without leaving a trace. The Bible, the commentator speculated, covered up the alien intervention by creating this myth about where all the languages came from.

Wait...what?

At the heart of the Christian worldview is this: The universe and everything in it was created by an Intelligent Designer who spoke life into existence out of nothing. God is the author of life; there was nothing before him, and everything originated with him.

Genesis 1:1–2 says this, "In the beginning God created the heavens and the earth. Now the earth was formless and empty, darkness was over the surface of the deep, and the Spirit of God was hovering over the waters."

This is very different from what I was told at school. When I attended public school during my elementary years, teachers taught us how the human race evolved from apes over billions of years. They told us each change was so minor that it took millions of years for each phase. They showed us the poster of an ape pictured on the left and gradually progressing into a man standing upright on the right side of the page.

Creation, on the other hand—they told us—has no scientific basis and should be treated as a fairytale. We are told that evolution is true, and creation is a myth. Regardless of the countless scientific discoveries during the past fifty years, evolution remains undisputed as fact in the public school system and elsewhere.

While attending Sunday School, however, I was told God created man in his own image and likeness. They taught us how Eve was created from a single rib out of Adam's side. As a child I remember seeing picture books showing the Garden of Eden and cartoon-like illustrations of the animals in full color. I believed that God created the universe and formed the human race on the sixth day of creation, but I also believed we evolved from apes, just as I was taught in elementary school.

Evolution, Smevolution

As I got older, I began to question evolution. If apes changed into men, then why are there still apes? Wouldn't there be half-ape/half-man creatures still out there? Why don't men continue to evolve today?

In my mind, it took a great leap of faith to believe that human beings could have evolved from apes.

The human race is, after all, much more complex than apes with greater motor skills, cognitive skills, and social skills. Even if I wanted to believe that man evolved from apes, I would have to concede that there was some form of intelligent design needed to engineer that impressive feat.

Throughout the centuries, men have invented elaborate stories and theories to explain away any theory that places God at the center. The most notorious of these men was Charles Darwin. Since his "scientific" theory of evolution is so widely accepted as truth, I was amazed to discover that Charles Darwin was not a biologist.

Not only was Charles Darwin not a biologist, but he didn't have a degree in any scientific field. Darwin originally went to Edinburgh University in Scotland to study medicine but realized that he couldn't handle the sight of blood. Instead, he changed his major to Theology. He had a Master of Arts, not science.

Rather than becoming a doctor, Darwin served as a clergyman in the Church of England. Darwin served in ministry for several years, until the unthinkable happened. In 1831 Darwin watched his ten-year-old daughter Annie suffer from disease and die a slow, painful death. As a result, he found it impossible to believe that an all-powerful God could allow such a thing and concluded that God did not exist.

His anti-God bias and rejection of God paved the way for the development of Darwin's evolution theory.

Even though evolution is a framework built on assumptions which never had and never will have direct, first-hand, observational proof, Darwinism has been uncontested in many circles, such as the public school system throughout America.

It's my conviction that is takes more blind faith to believe in evolution than to believe in creation. I personally think that it's intellectually dishonest to believe that we morphed in a transformer-like fashion from large, hairy apes. For me, it's easier to believe

God is the Intelligent Designer who created the universe and made mankind in his image and likeness.

God's power is clearly demonstrated through creation. "For since the creation of the world God's invisible qualities—his eternal power and divine nature—have been clearly seen, being understood from what has been made, so that people are without excuse" (Romans 1:20 NIV).

Here's the bottom line: No one knows with certainty what happened since neither creation nor evolution is observable or repeatable. As much as we would like to believe that we know the truth, empirical science can't definitively prove either the creation or the evolution theory.[5] Consequently, every single person—even those deemed to be experts in the field—allow personal biases to dictate where the evidence takes us.

Creation Theory is Good Science

There are many compelling reasons to believe the science behind creation and reject evolution.

> In the beginning was the Word, and the Word was with God, and the Word was God. He was with God in the beginning. Through him all things were made; without him nothing was made that has been made. In him was life, and that life was the light of all mankind (John 1:1–4).

Many reputable scientists agree that there is solid science behind creation theory and the existence of an Intelligent Designer.

There are several biological puzzles which continue to stump evolutionists such as 1) how do you get life from nonlife; 2) where did the information of life come from; and 3) how do you explain irreducible complexity.[6] These questions can't be answered by evolutionary theory, but make perfect sense within the Christian worldview. Let's explore these...

1. How Can You Make New Living Things?

You can't "make" living things. We can't give life to inanimate objects or invent new living things. Think about this: the world's most brilliant engineers can build a spaceship to travel to the moon but cannot successfully recreate an organism so basic as the housefly. Think about that...man can't even make a fly.

Even in the case of a tree "being made" from a seed, the seed was originally produced by a similar tree. It can develop into the same type of tree because the seed carries the identical genetic material as the original plant.

In fact, no mechanism by which non-living matter can randomly spark itself into life has ever been demonstrated.

Why, then, did Darwin's evolution theory conclude that man evolved from apes? I learned in college that Darwin published *On the Origin of Species by Means of Natural Selection* based on his observation of birds on the Galápagos Islands off the coast of Ecuador in

1859. He was forced to publish his book early because a competitor was ready to publish his own work on the same subject. He was still searching for the answers to how evolution occurred until his death. The truth is that he never found the answer to his question of how the species originated.

Darwin even states in his book that evolution occurred only in small steps, not big leaps. He went as far as to say that "if it could be demonstrated that any complex organism existed, which could not possibly have been formed by numerous, successive, slight modifications, my theory would absolutely break down."[7]

So, Darwin even admitted that his theory was fake news.

Evolution offers no answer for how life originated, but the idea of life from non-life is consistent with the account found in Genesis 1: "God spoke into existence the earth, the sky, sea, and everything that lives there."

It's my observation that every attempt to remove God from the equation results in some loose ends and a whole lot of chaos.

2. Who Programmed the Computer of Life?

Life consists of more than all the physical parts working in unison—it requires the information to run the parts. Think of it in terms of a computer. The computer is just a piece of hardware. The software must be engineered to communicate with the hardware in order for it to be useful.

There are 37 trillion cells in the human body which consist of 6 million nitrogen bases in each strand of DNA. And if, at conception, one single nitrogen base is not copied right, the person could suffer a defect as severe as having holes in their heart.

When you look at the complexity of a single strand of DNA, it would be very difficult to conclude that this could happen randomly. That would be like a toddler pounding on a piano keyboard and creating Beethoven's Symphony No. 9. Someone had to write the program for the human race.

This observation begs the question—where did this information come from? The simple truth is that biologists cannot determine where the "information of life" originated. Many modern scientists consider themselves to be materialists. Materialism is defined by Merriam-Webster as "a theory that physical matter is the only or fundamental reality and that all being and processes and phenomena can be explained as manifestations or results of matter."[8]

In other words, if you can't touch it, smell it, or see it...it's not real.

This may sound like a legitimate argument until you begin to think deeper. A true materialist rejects the idea that anything exists that cannot be proven. Nothing can exist outside "the box." Let's use the example of DNA mentioned above. We know that a single microscopic strand contains 6 million nitrogen bases. Where did the nitrogen bases come from? There's no rational explanation of how they appeared other than they were "created."

Materialism reminds me of a Looney Tunes cartoon I used to watch as a kid with the Roadrunner and Wile E. Coyote. The coyote would relentlessly chase the roadrunner, but to no avail. Every time Wile E. Coyote was close to catching the fast-running ground cuckoos, the Roadrunner would escape capture... *every time*. In the same way, the materialist reaches outside of "the box" of what he can see, touch, and feel. At some point the materialist falls off the cliff because he can't explain what happens next.

Once again, the Bible offers the only logical explanation for this...

> Through him [God] all things were made; without him nothing was made that has been made. In him was life, and that life was the light of all mankind. The light shines in the darkness, and the darkness has not overcome it (John 1:2–5).

3. Who Created the Creator?

As a child I remember asking the question of who created God. After all, how is it possible that He just appeared one day out of thin air? This was just one of the many ways I made my mom crazy as a child. As I got older, I realized this is exactly what happened. Our finite human minds—even as adults—cannot comprehend any person, place, or thing without a beginning or end.

"In the beginning the Word already existed. The Word was with God, and the Word was God" (John 1:1).

All of creation begs the idea of a Creator—an Intelligent Designer who spoke everything into existence from nothingness.

The scientific explanation for this is captured in what is known as the Theory of Irreducible Complexity. This theory states that there are certain organisms that randomly appeared that are so complex, but no one has an explanation for who created those organisms.[9]

Del Tackett, author of *The Truth Project* describes it this way: if you are walking through the forest and come across a wristwatch, you intrinsically know that someone created that watch. Because of the observed complexity, a reasonable individual concludes the watch did not grow out of the weeds.[10]

As I said earlier, it's my contention that it takes more blind faith [trust] to be an atheist than to believe that there was an Intelligent Designer that created everything from nothing.

Animal Kingdom

As I learned in middle school, the scientific community has attempted to classify the animal world into different groups. You may remember the terms species, genus, family, order, class, phylum, kingdom, and domain but scientists are constantly rethinking those classifications. Researchers can't even completely agree on the definition of the terms.

Unlike the man-made terms, the word "kind" as it relates to the animal kingdom in the Bible has a very distinct and important meaning.

> And God said, "Let the water teem with living creatures, and let birds fly above the earth across the vault of the sky." So God created the great creatures of the sea and every living thing with which the water teems and that moves about in it, according to their **kinds**, and every winged bird according to its **kind**. And God saw that it was good. God blessed them and said, "Be fruitful and increase in number and fill the water in the seas, and let the birds increase on the earth." And there was evening, and there was morning—the fifth day (Genesis 1:20–23).

The meaning of the term "kind" represents the basic reproductive boundary of an organism.[11] For example, cats and dogs are different kinds. However, a lion is in the cat family and thus the same kind.

What is fascinating is the potential for variation in each kind. Within a kind's DNA is the genetic material for a tremendous variety of different species. Scientists have suggested that an ordinary house cat may carry the genetic sequence for a lion, cheetah, jaguar, and more. When you consider this, the idea of Noah's ark doesn't sound so extreme. The ark wouldn't have needed to contain two of each species, just two of each kind.

It's true that the Creator of the universe allowed for enormous variety. At the same time, however, He also established boundaries within the animal kingdom to limit the development of new breeds. For example, a horse can mate with a donkey to produce a mule (because they are the same kind), but a horse can't mate with a giraffe, or an ostrich. And even when different species intermate, the product is typically sterile (as in the example of the mule—so that mule can't breed with another horse to create a... morse!).

Imagine the freak show that the animal kingdom would be if animals really could evolve into different species. We would conceivably have creatures with lion heads and alligator bodies. Evolution of species is a myth, but the development of the vast animal kingdom can be explained by creation.

Things that Go "Bang"

The big bang theory suggests that the universe began with an explosion causing particles to join together to create objects over the next billions of years to form the cosmos that we observe today.[12]

Consider this...*If there were to be an explosion in a brick factory, would you end up with skyscraper?* As ridiculous as that sounds, it's essentially what this theory is saying. I've watched the demolition of buildings and have never seen an explosion produce anything but rubble and dust.

Nowhere in the universe do we witness structure coming from randomness. Chaos does not naturally lead to order without purposeful planning and intervention. I can attest to the fact that if I neglect to clean my house, it gets more cluttered, not less.

Even if all of those random particles resulting from a big bang were somehow to come together in a logical order, that would point to a Master Designer. Think about that one.

Again, it takes less faith to believe that God spoke the universe into existence and… bang! There it was.

The Wrap-Up

Evolution is not a proven science but rather a scapegoat. When scientists can't find an explanation for abnormalities, they use the evolutionary theory to explain it away, rather than using evidence to explain evolutionary theory.[13]

Science and religion are not in opposition to each other. Faith in the historical accounts found in the Bible is not "blind" faith—it is supported by good science.

Now I realize that this is an oversimplification of a very complex subject and I'm no scientist, but then again, neither was Darwin.

DISCUSSION GUIDE

Chapter 2: In the Beginning

The purpose of this section is to help you facilitate a meaningful discussion surrounding the material in this chapter. Please refer to Appendix: Tips for Leading Small Group Discussions.

1. What, if anything, do you remember being taught in grade school about evolution or creation?

2. What do you believe about the formation of the universe? Explain why.

3. Explain in your own words how the term "kind" is used in the Bible?

4. Do you agree with the statement "science and religion are not opposed to each other"? Explain why or why not.

5. Do you agree with the big bang theory? Explain why or why not.

6. Were you surprised to discover that Charles Darwin was not a scientist?

Scriptures to read and discuss:

• Genesis 1 (entire chapter)

• Proverbs 8:22–31

• John 1:1–3

• Psalm 33:6

A video on this subject called "Did we Really Evolve from Apes" is available on the FUSION Leadership Group Site: https://www.fusionleadership.site/toughquestion-series

The Truth About Love

Awe...love. Who doesn't like to talk about love?
Think about how many songs have been sung,
movies shot, and books written on the subject. Love is oftentimes portrayed as that warm fuzzy
feeling we have when we have a deep emotional connection with another individual with whom we are
physically attracted. Without the romanticizing of love
there would be no Valentine's Day, no red roses, and
no Hallmark movies.

Love, after all, is meant to be the trademark of a
Christian. John 13:35 says, "Your love for one another
will prove to the world that you are my disciples."

Many of us have understood since we were young
that the greatest commandment—after loving God—is
to love your neighbor as yourself.

> One of the teachers of the law came and heard
> them debating. Noticing that Jesus had given
> them a good answer, he asked him, "Of all the

commandments, which is the most important?" "The most important one," answered Jesus, "is this: 'Hear, O Israel: The Lord our God, the Lord is one. Love the Lord your God with all your heart and with all your soul and with all your mind and with all your strength.' The second is this: 'Love your neighbor as yourself.' There is no commandment greater than these" (Matthew 28–31).

But, it's not as easy as it sounds.

I think it's fair to say that for many of us as believers in Jesus Christ, we have not always done a great job of loving each other. Love is an easy concept to talk about, but difficult to practice. Horrific things have been done through the centuries in the name of God that don't look anything like love.

Within our own culture we've been criticized as Christians for being judgmental. Some of this criticism is valid. I know that I've been guilty as charged at times. We would all do well to remember that we are broken people. None of us are perfect and we "all sin and fall short of the Glory of God."[14] Keeping this perspective would go a long way in building trust and repairing broken relationships.

Love Ain't

I wish it were always that simple, but it's not. Love has become a complicated topic in our culture. Like many concepts and institutions in our day, the idea of "love" and "hate" have been hijacked. The words are the same, but the uses of the words have dramatically changed. If we're not paying attention, we may start to believe that the truth surrounding these words have changed, too.

The problem is that secular worldviews dominating our culture are rejecting God and the idea of Truth in a spectacular way. When you remove the idea of absolute Truth from the equation, it becomes a free-for-all. Having even the *thought* of the Christian worldview in regard to love and sexuality—even if you don't verbalize it—is considered by some to be a "hate crime." The gloves come off when Christians attempt to hold their ground on biblical truth regarding the subject of love.

However, not all expressions of an opposing opinion are "hate" and not all sexual acts are "love." We'll discuss that more in a minute.

Kind of Love

The good news is that, even though love may have a different meaning, kindness and compassion have never gone out-of-style. Regardless of one's definition of love, kindness still looks the same.

We can all express kindness and compassion. Often, this is something that doesn't cost us anything.

One of the most famous Scriptures about love comes from 1 Corinthians 13:4–7:

> Love is patient and kind. Love is not jealous or boastful or proud or rude. It does not demand its own way. It is not irritable, and it keeps no record of being wronged. It does not rejoice about injustice but rejoices whenever the truth wins out. Love never gives up, never loses faith, is always hopeful, and endures through every circumstance.

Some simple ways to show kindness include smiling and laughing more, using common courtesies like saying please and thank you, giving a compliment, encouraging someone else who's in a tough spot, and speaking gently. Kindness can also be accomplished through listening—often for a long time—to someone who's lonely and may need a little extra attention.

How we handle ourselves on social media speaks volumes to our kindness or lack thereof.

We typically think of kindness as acts. However, kindness can be omissions, too. This can mean holding back on verbalizing something that we are thinking. Being kind can mean demonstrating patience with an individual or situation that is particularly frustrating. Refusing to retaliate—in words or actions—can build trust and bridge gaps that could not otherwise be overcome.

There are some not-so-simple ways of showing kindness, too. Offering forgiveness when someone has hurt, offended, or violated us, can be one of the greatest acts. When we refuse to forgive, we are holding onto debts that will never come due. It's a lesson in futility. Forgiveness is an exceptional way to show love.

Kindness is a language that transcends all barriers.

Compassion is similar to kindness but requires a deeper commitment. Demonstrating compassion takes more of your heart, mind, strength, and resources. Compassion can be investing in under-served communities, donating your time to worthy causes, or helping widows and orphans. Rather than a passing thought, this is usually a cause for which you have an emotional connection.

In 2019, I was with a group of individuals visiting a school/orphanage in Kagadi, Uganda, in East Africa. We had just spent all day with the four-hundred-plus kids at the school, and we were exhausted. Milly, my good friend and co-director of the school, insisted that she take us into the village to meet with some of the families of the children.

We stopped by the local market to buy food and supplies to take to the families. When we arrived in the village, I saw something I have never seen in my life...a community that did not have access to clean water! The children were beautiful, but very dirty and some were obviously sick. I discovered later that these ailments, such as having crossed-eyes like one of the four-year-old girls suffered from, was a result of the parasites in their contaminated water source.

Several of the kids from the school weren't there when we arrived in the village because they were off gathering water. They walked the three kilometers to and from school, and then had to walk another five kilometers to gather water for their families. The consequences of not being able to walk into the kitchen and turn on the faucet are far more extreme than I would have ever imagined.

Even after I returned home from that trip, I didn't forget the look on the faces of the children and adults as they struggled to survive. This was something I couldn't "unsee" as it was now permanently etched in my mind. This experience led us on a journey to help the rural communities in Uganda gain access to clean water. By partnering with an organization in Pittsburgh, we've been able to drill water wells in the very communities we visited!

Compassion is like kindness on steroids. It drives us to help others in ways we wouldn't think were possible. Compassion has the capacity to change lives, communities, and the world.

Loving the Truth

The truth about love is that—much to the dismay of many—it's not a blanket stamp of approval on all and every lifestyle choice. While it's important that we are tolerant and respectful of ALL people, we can love them without loving their life choices. We can love and appreciate someone without buying into their idea of reality. It's a difficult distinction to make, but a critical one.

The biblical concept of love is inextricably tied to truth. The two cannot be separated. Real, authentic love can only happen when combined with truth. Look again at 1 Corinthians 13:6: "Love does not delight in evil but rejoices with the truth."

Truth without love is cruelty, but love without truth is perversion. And the absence of both love and truth is deception.

Many people in the world today are expressing *neither* love nor truth. Anger and bitterness have replaced peace and civility. They are being deceived into thinking that good is evil and evil is good. They are being lied to by Satan, the father of lies.

These individuals are being gaslighted. Gaslighting, as defined by Britannica is an elaborate and insidious technique of deception and psychological manipulation. Its effect is to gradually undermine the victim's confidence in his own ability to distinguish truth from falsehood, right from wrong, or reality from appearance.[15] Satan has lied to us so often and for so long that it's hard to recognize the truth. He's the original gaslighter.

> The biblical concept of love is inextricably tied to truth. The two cannot be seperated.

Satan's purpose is to kill, steal, and destroy (John 10:10), but God created love and wants us to love each other in the spirit of truth.

Love is the Answer

The gap between the Christian worldview and others has never been wider. There's a great divide in our country right now, not necessarily between people who look differently, but between people who *think* differently. How can we show love and concern for those who may hate us? How can we reach people and authentically love people who think differently than us, without compromising our message?

Jesus provided a great model when He walked the earth. As I read through the gospels, I see the following pattern emerge: 1) Build the relationship; 2) Meet the need; 3) Address the sin.

Jesus showed incredible grace and patience for those who appeared to have lost their way in this life. The convicted thief, the addicted prostitute, the serial adulterer, the fraudulent embezzler, and even the rehabilitated murderer all received more of Jesus' time, attention, and compassion than nearly anyone else in New Testament accounts. At the same time, Jesus didn't condone or even overlook their bad choices or sinful lifestyles. He offered them care, compassion, and grace. But He also offered them truth.

How can we follow the same example?

1. Build the Relationship. It sounds very cliché, but people do not care about what you know until they know you care. If we're going to love people, particularly those who don't share our religious, political, or social views, we have to establish a personal relationship with them. Rather than arguing over social media, engage an individual one-on-one.

Relationships are hard work and can get messy, but they are a necessary step in showing care and compassion.

Jesus showed compassion and care for individuals, regardless of their ethnicity, political views, gender, or religious persuasion. We see specific examples in the Bible of when He healed an opposing soldier's daughter (Luke 7:1–10); touched and healed the man with an infectious disease (Matthew 8:3); saved a prostitute from abuse and ridicule (John 8:1–11); had dinner with a man who was a known thief (Luke 19:1–10); and had a deep conversation with a bi-racial woman as He was passing through hostile territory (John 4:1-26).

2. Meet the Need. If we are to have influence with individuals in our world, we have to look beyond the obvious and external appearances. Wealth, possessions, or attitudes can oftentimes conceal true needs. Needs don't have to be financial or material; someone can be crying for attention or connection. Love isn't a feeling, it's an action. If we are to truly love people and accept them for who they are, we need to invest our time, our affection, and often our resources. Helping others in need can be exhausting and expensive, but it's crucial if we're going to show others the love of Jesus.

We won't know the need, of course, until we establish the relationship first. Even though Jesus always knew their need, He made them ask for his help. I often wondered why that was. Obviously, the blind man needed his sight and the paraplegic needed to be able to walk again. What I've discovered, though, is that some individuals don't want help. They don't want to be healed. The more we try to meet a need that they don't think they have, the more they will reject the help—and us.

Jesus asked what they wanted as confirmation that they were ready to receive help. I've learned this the hard way. I've tried to help individuals get a job, buy a car, or start a business, just to discover that I wanted this for them more than they wanted it for themselves.

Other times, people tried to convince me of their dire need requiring my immediate attention (and money). On further inspection, there was no real need. Sometimes this individual was looking for an easy way out, but other times I was being scammed. Unfortunately, I've learned this one the hard way, too.

Until we *really* know their need, we can't meet it. Resist the urge to assume you know what another individual needs, even if it's a close friend or family member. You know what happens when we assume...

But once we know the real need, make every effort to address it. We also know what is said about the road to hell and how it's paved with good intentions.

3. *Address the Sin.* This is the tricky part of the equation. We live in a society where we're made to believe that "anything goes." Everyone gets to decide their own truth, so they tell us. What's right for you isn't right for me, they tell us. We are considered by many to be haters or judgmental if we even think about expressing our opinion. If we dare to speak out on social media about biblical truth, we are "canceled," or our message is labeled as hate speech.

Unfortunately, as I mentioned earlier, some of this bad press is well deserved. Often our tendency as Christians is to go directly to calling out the sin. When we do this, it becomes more about our own self-righteousness and less about concern for the other person. It helps me to remember that it is the job of the Holy Spirit to convict someone of their sin, not mine.

After Jesus saved a woman caught in the act of adultery, He told her, "now go and sin no more" (John 8:11). He also told a young man who was healed at the Pool of Bethesda to stop sinning (John 5:14). Wasn't that cruel for Jesus to tell them to stop sinning? No, it wasn't. He understood the consequences of their actions. He healed them from their physical ailments, but they had to choose to stop bringing more pain on themselves.

The bottom line is that speaking the truth in a kind, respectful way IS an act of love. Our culture is spiraling deeper and deeper into hopelessness and despair. In a culture that believes that it doesn't matter "who you love," this is a difficult position to take.

We don't have to blindly buy into everything that our culture is selling as love. God doesn't want us to live in isolation; He created relationships and established boundaries around them for our protection. In recent days, for example, one evidence of this distortion is the attempt in recent days to normalize pedophilia (sexual acts with children)! How can we stand by and not take a stand for truth?

It's not kind to allow people to suffer from the consequences of bad choices without offering them hope, help, and the truth. The apostle Paul said, "You say, 'I am allowed to do anything'—but not everything is good for you. You say, 'I am allowed to do anything'—but not everything is beneficial" (1 Corinthians 10:23-24).

God, in his infinite wisdom, gave us free will to make any choice we would like, but He also provided boundaries to show us which choices are in our best interest. As believers in Jesus, we have an obligation to speak truth to our friends and family whose poor choices are causing chaos in their lives and those around them.

We don't need to be rude or abrasive, but we can't ignore the consequences of destructive behavior, either. Let's show love and respect for everyone, regardless of who they are, what they believe, or how they act.

Love You... More

We express our love to others when we show kindness and compassion. But we also show love by sharing the good news of the gospel. Yes, we may offend people when we share the truth in love, but it's worth the risk if we truly care about them.

God continues to show us how to love those around us by how much He loves you and me. God loves you so much that He sent his only Son to suffer and die... for you![16] God calls us his children, assures us that nothing can separate us from his love, and promises eternity in his presence for those who believe in his Son Jesus. Until we can grasp the depth of God's love for us, it will be a challenge for us to love others.

The truth is—the more we learn to love God with all of our heart and with all of our soul and with all of our strength, the more we will be able to authentically love others, especially those we don't agree with.

DISCUSSION GUIDE

Chapter 3: The Truth About Love

The purpose of this section is to help you facilitate a meaningful discussion surrounding the material in this chapter. Please refer to Appendix: Tips for Leading Small Group Discussions.

1. Can you summarize the main idea of this chapter?

2. What does the psychological term "gaslighter" mean? How is Satan the original gaslighter?

3. What is the difference between kindness and compassion? What are some personal ways that you have shown either kindness or compassion?

4. In the section "Love is the Answer," what are the three steps the author uses to describe the model Jesus used to express both love and truth?

5. Can you give a personal example of when you've had to speak the truth in love?

6. The author states, "The more we learn to love God with all of our heart and with all of our soul and with all of our strength, the more we will be able to authentically love others." Do you agree that it is difficult to love other people if we don't first love God? Why or why not?

Scriptures to read and discuss:
- 1 Corinthians 13:4–5
- 1 John 4:16
- Ephesians 4:2
- 1 Corinthians 16:14
- Romans 12:9

For Heaven's Sake

Several years ago, I read an article about boxing legend Cassius Clay. Clay converted to Islam in 1972 after winning the heavyweight boxing title and changed his name to Muhammad Ali. When he was drafted into the US Army during the Vietnam era, he refused to go because of religious reasons. This is typically acceptable, but Ali repeatedly antagonized the government by saying that he would fight in the war if—and only if—Allah told him to. Ali was arrested for desertion, but later released on a technicality.

At the time I read this article, Ali was still alive but barely able to speak because of the brain damage from multiple head traumas. His brother was interviewed about the former champ's declining health. He made an interesting statement about his brother's fate.

"He's going to heaven, there's no doubt," Rahman Ali said. "If his funeral was tomorrow, all the statesmen of the world would turn up. He touched everyone from the rich to the poor."[17]

Wait. Did his brother just claim that Ali's popularity was the golden ticket to get him into heaven? That's not what Islam teaches, or any other religion for that matter.

What happens after we die? Since no one has died and lived to tell about it, we don't know for sure. Unfortunately, many people have opinions about the afterlife which are not based on evidence, facts, or even educated opinions. The best we can do is to look to respected sources to find the truth. The Bible is very clear about the pathway to heaven, and we'll discuss that further throughout the chapter.

When it comes to the path to heaven, it's important to note that in the end someone is going to be right, and someone is going to be wrong. The tragic problem is that by the time we figure out if we guessed correctly or not, it's too late.

Heaven Help Us

God created human beings with a "God vacuum." This is the space that can only be fulfilled and completed through a personal relationship with the God of the universe. When people reject the knowledge of God, it creates a vacuum that must be filled with something else. This is one reason many people struggle with addictions. We probably all know of people who have attempted to use drugs, alcohol, food, sex, or whatever else to numb the pain and fill the void.

Others, however, attempt to use *religion* to fill that void. As hard as it may be to believe, religion can actually keep people from finding the truth. That was a difficult concept for me to grasp at first.

Religions exist because we were born with a desire for knowledge that God placed in all of mankind. God created us with a burning desire to know him.

It is important that we recognize that religion does not point the way to eternal life, only Jesus does. And in fact, many religious systems attempt to find a way around Jesus' redemptive work on the cross by replacing the free gift of salvation with a list of do's and don'ts. This is based on the assumption that we can work our way into heaven.

Religions are theories made by man, but biblical Christianity is divinely inspired. Religion makes you work for your salvation. But in Christianity, Jesus paid for your salvation. All you have to do is accept his free gift.

Think of it this way: Religion is like that crash-diet that we've all been on in the past. We starve our-selves in hopes of losing weight quickly. We're always checking the scale and counting the calories. It's ok for a while, but then the cracks start to show. We start dreaming about gorging on chocolate cake. We wake up and think about eating all day long. Before we know it, we're bingeing on cake, ice cream, potato chips, pizza, and all those things we were trying so desperately to avoid.

Christianity is more like the exercise plan where we start slowly. Instead of becoming fixated on the results, we focus on the process. We concentrate on becoming healthier by making subtle, small choices. Pretty soon we feel better physically, so we start eating better. As the results begin to show and our friends begin to comment on the positive changes, we are more inspired to work harder.

> Religion does not point the way to eternal life, only Jesus does.

In Christianity, the process is to focus on our relationship with Jesus. The more we concentrate on learning about him and reading the instruction manual He left for us—the Bible— the more we want to know about him. The gains come in small increments, but soon we learn to think and act more like Jesus. We begin to understand that getting to heaven isn't the main objective, it's our reward for accepting the free gift of Jesus.

But admittedly, the church as a whole and Christians individually haven't always done a great job of making Christianity attractive and inviting. I've talked to a lot of people who don't have a problem with Jesus, but they aren't fans of the church. Please understand that all religious institutions are flawed and will continue to be, as long as human beings are involved.

Many of us would like to think that our idea about what happens after we die is true for us, even if it's not true for others. We think that any belief—as long as it's sincere—will get us to heaven. Here's the problem with the idea that all roads lead to heaven: it's based on a false assumption. We picture God passively sitting on the top of a mountain and it doesn't matter which path we take; we just have to climb up to reach him. But, according to the Bible, Jesus is coming down one path to meet us. If we take any other path up the mountain, we will miss him.

The fact that God determines the path to heaven—not us—is clearly seen in the claims of Jesus:

- "Jesus said, 'I am the Way the Truth and the Light, no one comes to the Father except through me'" (John 14:6).

- "Enter through the narrow gate. For wide is the gate and broad is the road that leads to destruction, and many enter through it" (Matthew 7:13).

- "My Father's house has many rooms; if that were not so, would I have told you that I am going there to prepare a place for you? And if I go and prepare a place for you, I will come back and take you to be with me that you also may be where I am" (John 14:2–3).

Six Degrees of Separation

I want to discuss six ways in which Christianity is separate from other religions:

First, *Jesus is the only one who provided for our salvation and acceptance into his kingdom.*

Jesus paid the price for our salvation so that we don't have to. If you look closely at some of the more common world religions, Buddha, Allah, and others never promised to save us. But Jesus came to earth just as we do—as an innocent baby—to do just that. He grew and learned about life in the same way we do. The Bible says that Jesus was tempted in the same ways we are, but He remained faithful to his Father so that He could prepare the way to heaven for us.[18]

I didn't realize it until I studied it in college, but Hinduism claims to have thirty-three million gods. Unfortunately, not a single one of those gods can save us from anything.

Contrast this with Jesus' sacrificial death on the cross. He paved the way to paradise for us. Jesus did all of the hard word for our salvation.

> God saved you by his grace when you believed. And you can't take credit for this; it is a gift from God. Salvation is not a reward for the good things we have done, so none of us can boast about it (Ephesians 2:8–9).

Second, *compassion is unique to Christianity and is explicitly connected to the person of Jesus.*

Jesus' compassion is seen throughout his time on earth. He healed those who were sick and broken; He fed those who were starving; He showed kindness to those who were disenfranchised; He protected those who were vulnerable; He engaged those who were ostracized; and He forgave those who abused and even tortured him. Matthew 11:28–30 says:

Come to me, all you who are weary and burdened and I will give you rest. Take my yoke upon you. Let me teach you, because I am humble and gentle at heart, and you will find rest for your souls. For my yoke is easy to bear, and the burden I give you is light.

Suffering, as we'll see in the next chapter, is a central part of the human experience. Because Jesus lived on earth and experienced the same heartbreak and misery as us, He can relate to our pain. I find it telling that some world religions don't acknowledge suffering. Unfortunately, these religious systems can't offer us any help or relief from our pain.

Third, *the Creator of the universe desires a personal relationship with us and extends the invitation to all.*

The God of creation sent his only Son to suffer and die a painful, humiliating death on the cross so that YOU AND I could live forever with him in heaven. He loves us so much—even when we reject him—that He continues to pursue a personal relationship with each one of us. Other religious systems don't offer a personal connection to God. In fact, often we find an "Us-vs-Them" mentality.

God loves you and me so much that He is delaying his return to earth so as many as possible can be saved (see 2 Peter 3:9).

Fourth, *Jesus is the only (sane) person who ever claimed to be God.*

No one else has ever claimed to be both God and man. We know that Allah was not a real person and Siddhartha Gautama (later known as Buddha) never claimed to be anything but a man. Jesus not only claimed to be God but proved it when He rose again after being crucified and dying a slow, painful death.

If Jesus was just a good man or a prophet, He would have been lying. This is a critical distinction because, since Jesus—as God—is the only one who can save us. If we don't believe that Jesus is God, then we would have to work for our salvation, as religion tells us.

Fifth, *the Bible is the only sacred book that was divinely written and preserved.* The Bible was written over a period of three thousand years by forty different authors from three different continents and using three different languages. It is the only book of its kind that has <u>no</u> known discrepancies with history, archeology, astronomy, or any other area of science. There is more written, secular (non-biblical) evidence to prove Jesus Christ was a real person who walked the earth than there is to prove that Napoleon existed.

This is vastly different than what we know about the Qur'an. We know that the Qur'an was written over a period of twenty-three years. The Qur'an is only meant to be understood in classic Arabic, even though 80% of the Muslim population doesn't know Arabic. Furthermore, the prophet Muhammad was the only person to whom Allah ever appeared.[19]

The fact that the narratives in the Bible have been collaborated by many individuals on different continents, using different languages, and over thousands of years, is truly amazing. Documents, known now as the Dead Sea Scrolls, were discovered between 1947 and 1956 in eleven different caves on the shore of the Dead Sea in Israel. These documents date back to over two thousand years ago! This chapter is just a brief overview and doesn't give us enough room to talk about what a miracle it is that the Bible was preserved in this way.[20]

And sixth, *the concept of heaven as recorded in Scripture is unique to Christianity.*

Not only do all religions not lead to heaven; many religions don't claim to.

In Buddhism, death is an end to the suffering in life. The name Nirvana literally means "blown out," as in a candle.[21]

In Hinduism, one must continually be reincarnated up the scale until one simply ceases to exist. If an individual was bad in this present life, they would be reincarnated as a lower form and have to work harder in that lifetime to be reincarnated as a higher form in the future.

Islam uses the term heaven, but it sounds very different than the picture of heaven given in the Bible.

Contrast those definitions with the description found in Revelation 21:18–27:

> The wall [of heaven] was made of jasper, and the city of pure gold, as pure as glass. The foundations of the city walls were decorated with every kind of precious stone. The first foundation was jasper, the second sapphire, the third agate, the fourth emerald, the fifth onyx, the sixth ruby, the seventh chrysolite,

the eighth beryl, the ninth topaz, the tenth turquoise, the eleventh jacinth, and the twelfth amethyst [these last two stones are unknown or only exist in heaven today]. The twelve gates were twelve pearls, each gate made of a single pearl. The great street of the city was of gold, as pure as transparent glass. I did not see a temple in the city, because the Lord God Almighty and the Lamb are its temple. The city does not need the sun or the moon to shine on it, for the glory of God gives it light, and the Lamb is its lamp. The nations will walk by its light, and the kings of the earth will bring their splendor into it. On no day will its gates ever be shut, for there will be no night there. The glory and honor of the nations will be brought into it. Nothing impure will ever enter it, nor will anyone who does what is shameful or deceitful, but only those whose names are written in the Lamb's book of life.

Heaven is a beautiful, glorious place where God will reign forever, and there will be no pain, suffering, or death. It's not simply an end to our suffering on earth, it is a new life for all of eternity.

The Wrap Up

The short answer to "do all roads lead to heaven?" is no; hell no. Jesus is the only way to spend eternity with God in heaven. There are no shortcuts, *no passing Go and no collecting $200.*

It's my observation that most people feel that they deserve to go to heaven, and so invent their own theology that will land them there without observing guidelines of any religion. It's the à la carte approach to salvation—take the viewpoints from the Bible you like and leave the rest behind. As difficult as it is for us to accept, according to the Bible, not everyone will enter heaven.

If you are reading this, though, you can make a choice *now* that will change your trajectory for all of eternity. I encourage you to drop any erroneous, fictious, made-up beliefs about how one gets to heaven and make a choice to believe that Jesus is the author and finisher of our faith. He is the only path to heaven. Romans 10:9 says, "If you openly declare that Jesus is Lord and believe in your heart that God raised him from the dead, you will be saved."

If you've already made this commitment, you have a responsibility to share the good news with the rest of mankind. Let's not allow our friends and family to buy into the illusion that they will go to heaven as long as they are sincere in their belief. Unless you and I hold the personal conviction that our friends and family are doomed to an eternity of torment and separation from God without the saving knowledge of Jesus Christ—and only Jesus Christ—our message and motivation for sharing the gospel will be compromised.

For heaven's sake...it doesn't matter what you believe, it only matters what is true.[22]

DISCUSSION GUIDE

Chapter 4: For Heaven's Sake

The purpose of this section is to help you facilitate a meaningful discussion surrounding the material in this chapter. Please refer to Appendix: Tips for Leading Small Group Discussions.

1. Can you summarize the main idea of this chapter?

2. What is your personal opinion or conviction about how one gets to heaven?

3. The author compares religion to crash-dieting. Explain why you agree or disagree.

4. Explain at least one of the six differences between Christianity and other religions mentioned in the "Six Degrees of Separation" section.

5. How do different religions describe heaven?

6. Do you have a personal relationship with Jesus Christ? Are you confident that you will spend all of eternity in heaven?

Scriptures to read and discuss:

- Psalm 32:8

- 2 Timothy 3:16

- John 14:6

- Matthew 7:13

- John 14:2–3

- 2 Peter 3:9

A video on this subject called "Do All Roads Lead to Heaven" is available on the FUSION Leadership Group Site: https:// www.fusionleadership.site/toughquestionseries

Making Sense of the Senseless

Questions. We all have them.

Recently I read a study stating that moms are asked an average of three hundred questions a day. This is more questions per hour than a teacher or a doctor receives per day! The research found that four-year-old girls were the most curious, asking 390 questions a day. That's an average of one question every two minutes.[23] This must be why our children are so smart (smile).

The questions don't stop as we get older; they just get harder. One of the hardest questions I've ever been asked is this: Why does God allow bad things to happen? This extraordinarily complex question deserves a very thoughtful and sensitive response. In fact, most of the time when this question has been posed to me, it was by someone who really wasn't looking for an answer, but rather seeking reassurance that even though their world was falling apart, they are going to be ok.

I've observed two common responses from people facing loss and tragedy: 1) They believe God is to blame for their suffering; and 2) They conclude that their pain is proof that God doesn't exist.

Despite the blatantly apparent contradiction, many people manage to hold both of these views at the same time.

It's understood that grief has a way of clouding our judgement and veiling reality, but please realize this: Just because you don't feel God's presence or see him working in your situation, that doesn't mean that He isn't there. Psalm 34:18 states, "The Lord is close to the brokenhearted; He rescues those whose spirits are crushed." Your suffering may have caused you to turn away from God, but it hasn't caused him to turn from you.

Contrary to popular opinion, pain and suffering aren't proof that God is absent.

One of the first things I learned in my Apologetics class my freshman year of college was that *you can't prove a universal negative.* It would be like attempting to prove that there was no air. Think about that for a minute. It's impossible to prove the absence of anything. I personally don't think UFOs exist, but I can't prove it. Even though I have never seen a UFO, there is no way for me to empirically prove that they do not exist.

In the same way, a thousand skeptics couldn't convince one true believer that there is no God. It's impossible to prove a universal negative.

The Battle Rages

You may be saying yeah, but that still didn't answer my question. If God exists, why does He allow suffering?

It is foundational to the Christian worldview to understand the war between good and evil, and to acknowledge that we're standing in the middle of the battlefield. The Bible makes it clear that the devil is alive and well on planet Earth. Satan is our archenemy, and his plan is—and has always been—to rob, kill, and destroy (John 10:10).

Without this perspective, nothing that happens in this life will make sense to you.

Evil isn't just a mystical idea, either. In the same way that God chooses to work in and through us when we submit to the Holy Spirit, Satan uses people to spew his lies, hatred, and violence. We have been given the chance to choose between right and wrong, and our choices have consequences both here on earth and in eternity. We are warned as Christians not to "give the devil a foothold," or to allow Satan to influence our choices. As difficult as it can be for us to comprehend, people can be motivated and controlled by evil.

> Once you were dead because of your disobedience and your many sins. You used to live in sin, just like the rest of the world, obeying the devil—the commander of the powers in the unseen world. He is the spirit at work in the hearts of those who refuse to obey God (Ephesians 2:1–2).

The source of evil is not God's power, but man's freedom.[24]

The fact is we live in a fallen world. We cannot control the actions and choices of others, and as a result, we have all experienced the consequences of someone else's choices. It's not our fault, but we still pay the price. It's the downside to free will. Other times there are just tragedies that defy logic. Matthew 5:45 states, "[God] gives his sunlight to both the evil and the good, and He sends rain on the just and the unjust alike."

Yet, somehow, we think that the One who formed the vast galaxies, set each star in place, commands the waves of the ocean, and holds all of humanity in the palm of his hand owes us an explanation. I'm afraid that I will never understand when a child dies, or a good person suffers from a terrible illness, or when evil rears its ugly head. But I'm also spiritually mature enough to recognize the small-minded, humanness of my own thinking.

In October of 2019, our twenty-two-year-old nephew Josh was killed in a tragic accident. By all accounts he wasn't doing anything wrong, just driving to work. Josh was kind, had a great work ethic, and just an incredible young man with his whole life ahead of him.

I don't know why this happened, but one thing I know—God is sovereign. This is a great mystery to us mere mortals. In simple terms, God's sovereignty "is his right and power to do all that He decides to do."[25] I'll never understand, but I trust in God's goodness and mercy, even when I can't see it.

Cause and Effect

There are also some practical reasons why we experience pain and suffering. Unfortunately, some—though not all—are our own fault.

We don't like to admit it, but we've all experienced consequences of our own actions. I know I have. When I eat too much and don't exercise enough, I gain weight and my health suffers. When I drive too fast, I get a speeding ticket—and then my wallet suffers.

Even though I understand on an intellectual level that I cause a lot of my own troubles, it's easier to blame someone else. We prefer to call it "bad luck," or "being in the wrong place at the wrong time," or "the officer didn't like me," and on it goes. Some individuals make an art form out of blaming others. If there was an Academy Award for playing the victim, we all know people who would clean up in that category.

As mentioned earlier, we also like to blame God for our pain. We say "he's punishing me" because we see consequences as punitive. But this just isn't true. Consequences are not the same as punishments. Punishments are intended to embarrass, humiliate, hurt, or cause suffering, and are usually done out of anger.[26] Punishment has no redemptive value; it's meant to inflict pain and shame.

Does that sound like the God who sent his only Son to suffer and die so that we may spend all of eternity with him in heaven? Of course not. God loves you and has a plan and purpose for your life. He's not trying to punish or hurt you. Instead, God wants to guide and direct us, for our own benefit. Isaiah 48:17 says,

> This is what the Lord says—
> your Redeemer, the Holy One of Israel:
> "I am the Lord your God,
>   who teaches you what is good for you
>   and leads you along the paths you should
> follow."

Unlike punishment meant to inflict pain, natural consequences are the direct effect of our behavior. These may result in a negative physical, social, psychological, or spiritual outcome, such as burning our hand when we touch a hot surface, or being disciplined for breaking a rule, or feeling badly about a rude comment we made. Consequences can bring about positive change in our behavior because often they are warning signals that it is time to make a change.

Purpose in the Pain

Whether we realize it or not, pain is not the problem. Pain is an indication of the true problem. In 2012, my husband suffered a heart event. His left anterior descending artery (LAD)—also known as the "widowmaker" for the devastating impact a blockage in that artery can cause—was 99% obstructed! He was transported by ambulance to a local hospital and, within minutes, had two stints implanted. Thanks to the quick actions of the paramedics, skilled work of the cardiac surgeon, and the grace of God, He's still with us today.

When I tell the story, the common response is "oh that's awful." However, in the grand scheme of things, it wasn't awful. In fact, it was the best thing that could have happened. The heart attack was a warning sign that one of his main arteries was severely blocked. If he wasn't able to get immediate medical attention, he would have died from the blockage in his artery, not from the pain caused by the heart attack. It sounds like I'm splitting hairs here, but it's an important distinction to make.

Pain is not the enemy. On the contrary, God uses our pain as a powerful tool to get our attention.

The good news here is that we can save ourselves a lot of pain and suffering by following God's laws. As we discussed in Chapter 1, we didn't make the rules and we don't get to change them. The Creator of the universe designed a mechanism within human beings to be able to discern right from wrong, also known as our conscience. Romans 2:15 explains it this way:

> They demonstrate that God's law is written in their hearts, for their own conscience and thoughts either accuse them or tell them they are doing right." God gave us the ability to discern which things would cause us pain. If we ignore these warning signs, there is always a price to pay.

I remember talking with my friend Tina about the subject. We were on our way to a concert, and she was driving. I relayed to her something I recently heard on the radio (I don't even remember by whom). "Imagine how much heartache and pain would be avoided in the world if everyone would only have sex with their spouse. There would be no extramarital affairs, no children born out of wedlock, no rape, and no sexually transmitted diseases, among other things."

She was so shocked at this statement—having never considered it before—that she almost wrecked the car!

The moral guidance laid out in the Bible, including the Ten Commandments, are meant for our benefit. His game; His rules—and they don't change, regardless of public opinion. When God says "no, don't do that," what He's really saying to us is "this will hurt you." We can avoid a lot of unnecessary pain and heartache by following our God-given, internal compass.

It's difficult for us to understand that God doesn't view suffering in the same way that we do. We want to avoid it; we want it to go away; we want to pretend it doesn't exist. Sometimes we see our pain as proof that God is mad at us or doesn't care about us, but nothing could be further from the truth.

One of my favorite success stories is Norman Yoshio Mineta. He served as the Secretary of Commerce in the Clinton Administration and Secretary of Transportation in the Bush Administration. Mineta is the only individual to fill Cabinet positions for both the Republican and Democratic parties. But Mineta—born to Japanese immigrants—didn't rise to his position of influence in the typical way.

In 1941, Mineta was ten years old when the Japanese military attacked the US Naval base at Pearl Harbor. Following the horrific assault which killed over 2,400 American military personnel and civilians, Mineta was detained along with his parents at an internment camp for several years during the remainder of World War II.

Norman was a big baseball fan as a kid. But when he arrived at the camp with his prized possessions— his baseball bat and glove—the bat was confiscated by the authorities, citing that it could be used as a weapon.

This unfortunate series of events did not break his spirit, though. Mineta went on to graduate from the University of California with a degree in Business Administration and later served as an intelligence officer in the US Army in Japan and Korea. Mineta's introduction to politics came through his close friend, Alan Simpson, future US Senator from Wyoming. The two young men met when Simpson's Boy Scout troop would regularly visit the other Scouts, including Mineta, at the internment camp.

The parallels between Mineta's story and the account of Joseph in the Book of Genesis are remarkable. Joseph was sold as a slave by his insanely jealous older, half-brothers. He was trafficked out of his home country of Israel and taken to Egypt. Because of the betrayal at the hands of his brothers, Joseph faced isolation, persecution, and imprisonment. Through remarkable circumstances and God's favor, however, Joseph defied the odds and eventually became second-in-command in Egypt, second only to Pharaoh himself.

Remarkably, both Mineta and Joseph rose to power in government. There was not a natural path that either of these young men could take to arrive at their final destination. It took extraordinary, and even tragic circumstances to pave the way.

In fact, it's my personal conviction that there are very few pathways to success that do not originate, or at least travel through the valley of pain and suffering. G.K. Chesterton, a theologian from the 19th century explained it this way: "One sees great things from the valley; only small things from the peak."[27]

Joseph's misfortune and suffering eventually led him to a position where he oversaw the gathering and stockpiling of grain and other crops during the plentiful years. When a famine came seven years later, his leadership was responsible for saving the lives of thousands— including his brothers who had abandoned him years earlier.

Joseph understood that God had a plan, even when he thought He had abandoned him. In Genesis 50:20 he declares boldly to his brothers that "You intended to harm me, but God intended it all for good. He brought me to this position so I could save the lives of many people."

The Wrap Up

God, the author of life, didn't have to allow suffering. When you look closer you see that God not only permits it, but suffering is so central to the human experience that He sent his Son to earth to suffer and die. Jesus' redemptive work on the cross is more meaningful because of the pain and anguish He suffered—for our benefit.

Here's the remarkable thing about God—*He redeems our suffering.* He doesn't just allow it; He assigns purpose to it. He can transform the heartbreak and pain in our lives to benefit ourselves and others. Often, our pain becomes our platform.

But the choice is ours. We have the free will to choose to abide by God's moral code and save ourselves—and others—a lot of heartache and pain. Or we can give the devil a foothold in our lives.

Even when we experience consequences to our own poor choices, God doesn't give us what we deserve. We receive grace and mercy in place of punishment and condemnation. The short answer to why God allows bad things to happen (and we don't have to like it) is that evil and man's free will afford God the opportunity to demonstrate his love, grace, and mercy.

DISCUSSION GUIDE

Chapter 5: Making Sense of the Senseless

The purpose of this section is to help you facilitate a meaningful discussion surrounding the material in this chapter. Please refer to Appendix: Tips for Leading Small Group Discussions.

1. Can you summarize the main idea of this chapter?

2. What does the author say about "universal negatives"? Can you name one (other than the one mentioned in this chapter)?

3. What is meant by "pain is not the enemy"?

4. Talk about a time (if appropriate) when you suffered consequences for someone else's poor choices.

5. Talk about a time when you made a bad choice (again, please use discretion) and suffered for your actions.

6. Do you agree or disagree with the idea that "God can redeem our suffering"? Explain your position.

Scriptures to read and discuss:

- Hebrews 4:16
- 1 Peter 4:10
- Micah 6:8
- 1 John 1:9
- Deuteronomy 4:31
- Joel 2:12–14

A video on this subject entitled "Why Does God Allow Bad Things to Happen" is available on the FUSION Leadership Group Site: https://www.fusionleadership.site/toughquestionseries

Part II:
Game On

The Rights of Life

In December of 2006, I ran into a friend I hadn't seen in years at a local coffee shop. At the time, I had no idea the lasting impact that chance meeting would have. Susan (we'll call her), normally vibrant and happy, was really distraught that day. After a little small talk, she relayed the bad news she received that week. She and her husband had tried for years to have a baby, without success. Once the medical options were exhausted, a plan was finally in place to adopt a child through a local agency. They were scheduled to pick up the child the following week when they received the call—the birth mom changed her mind. After months and months of prayer and paperwork, when the end was in sight, their hope changed in an instant. Susan was crushed.

My heart hurt for my friend. Our third child was four years old at the time, and I couldn't imagine not being able to have children. I prayed for her that day, but there wasn't much else I could do.

Within a week of speaking with Susan, I ran into another friend. I saw this woman consistently and we often had brief conversations, usually about the weather and other unimportant stuff. On this day, Sandi (we'll call her) confided that she was in a tough spot: she was pregnant to a man she wasn't married to. She already had two children and couldn't imagine how she could care for a third. When she broke the news to her boyfriend, he ended the relationship and refused to see her.

Sandi held the conviction that abortion was not an option, so she was looking for someone to adopt her baby. A family member had originally agreed to adopt the child, but he and his wife had just backed out of the arrangement only days before we spoke.

As I listened, I tried hard not to jump out of my chair. After a while I told her that I knew someone who may want to adopt her baby and asked her permission to speak to my friend. If she was interested, I promised to connect them. Sandi was excited about the prospect and gave me permission to bring up the subject with my friend.

I will never forget making that call on Christmas Eve. It must have been hard to conceal my excitement because Susan later said she knew why I was calling, even before I told her. The two women met together shortly thereafter, and the rest is history. The baby girl born in June of 2007 was adopted by Susan and her husband. God had—once again—worked out a solution to the problem for all the women, even before they were aware of their dilemmas.

There are a lot of social issues in America today which the Bible doesn't have any direct answers, but the case for protecting innocent life isn't one of them. Genesis 1 proclaims that God made man in his image; Exodus 20 records the Sixth Commandment, "You must not murder"; and Psalm 139 declares boldly and beautifully how life begins at conception. Very severe warnings are given against those who would harm children in both the Old Testament and the New Testament. Luke 17:2, for example, states: "It would be better for them to be thrown into the sea with a millstone tied around their neck than to cause one of these little ones to stumble" (NIV).

There is no room for "gray area" in the Christian worldview regarding abortion.

One of the more perplexing divisions of our times is between those who promote abortion (women's choice) and those who advocate for life. In 1973, the now-famous United States Supreme Court case *Roe v. Wade* ruled that access to safe and legal abortion is a constitutional right. This legislation became an extension of the idea that government shouldn't be able to tell women what to do with their bodies. Ever since that time, a battle has ensued.

Because all life is deemed sacred by God, many have taken up the cause of protecting the unborn. The pro-life movement started and was fueled by the Catholic

Church which was among the first to recognize that life is a God-given privilege. In 1968, Pope Paul VI forbid abortion and most methods of birth control.[28]

Although this stance has been disputed in recent days, many within the Catholic Church still valiantly defend the rights of the unborn child. Sister Deirdre Bryne proudly represents the best of this community. In a speech she gave in August 2020 to a national audience, Sister Dede, a retired Army officer and surgeon, discussed her work serving the poor in Haiti, Sudan, Kenya, and Iraq. She talked about how the refugees she has worked with have been marginalized, viewed as insignificant, and have been deemed powerless.

The largest marginalized group in the world, though, Sister Dede stated, are not outside our borders. They are here in the United States and they are the unborn.[29]

Toward the end of the 1970s, evangelical Christians joined the movement.[30] As late as the 1960s, pastors and evangelical scholars couldn't agree if abortion was sinful. But thanks to the groundbreaking work done by our Catholic brothers and sisters, the sentiment changed. More and more evangelical organizations such as Students for Life of America, Concerned Women for America, the Family Research Council, and others joined the fight. For the next few decades, the focus shifted from saving babies at all costs, to educating and supporting women in crisis. During this time, the "face" of the movement changed to become characterized by white, suburban conservatives.

The *Roe v. Wade* legislation remained uncontested for several decades. But on October 2, 2003, under President George Bush, the Partial-Birth Abortion Ban Act was passed to ban certain procedures deemed to be cruel and barbaric. This decision marked the first time since 1973 that any restrictions were placed on abortion.[31]

In recent years, however, there has been a push to overturn the ban on late-term abortions. This legislation has been the only restraints on the annual US $1.3 billion industry.[32]

Rather than continued progress toward making abortion illegal, many proponents are choosing to double down. The push toward political correctness has caused the unthinkable murder of viable, unborn babies to become more acceptable. Some in the media seek to change what they deem to be the offensive labeling of "pro-choice" and "pro-life" to include more neutral phrases such "abortion-rights advocates" and "abortion-rights opponents."[33] Advocates for abortion on demand are offended by the term "pro-life," possibly because it implies that unborn children have rights, not just the activists.

Here is what I do not understand: Why isn't adoption being pushed as an alternative to late-term abortion? As a human being, partial-birth abortion doesn't make sense to me on any level. But as a mother, it makes even less sense. Why would any woman purposely go through nine months of pregnancy if they had even an inkling that they want to abort?

Pregnancy is no fun. I can't imagine any rational, caring woman willingly choosing to kill the child they carried for the past nine months, rather than seeking a plan for adoption.

You may not realize this if you've never had the need, but every state in the United Sates has Safe Haven laws. This means that a mother, and even a father, can relinquish an unharmed baby to any hospital without risk of being prosecuted for child abandonment. Many states have gone to great lengths to ensure privacy to protect both the child and the person relinquishing them.[34]

With so many other legitimate, legal, and humane options, why is late-term, partial-birth abortion still even up for discussion? This indicates to me that something else is at play in this situation.

The country's largest provider of abortions is the infamous organization, Planned Parenthood. If you go to the Planned Parenthood (PP) website, you'll read how the organization was founded in 1916 on the idea that women should have "the information and care they need to live strong, healthy lives, and fulfill their dreams."[35] This notion is easily debunked, however, when you begin to investigate further.

I remember being shown a video in fifth grade from Planned Parenthood demonstrating how women "have a choice." I will never forget coming home and telling my mom, very nonchalantly, about the woman in the video. When told by the doctor that she was having a girl, she immediately declared that she wanted an abortion because she already had two girls. The doctor agreed that this was a good option and scheduled her appointment.

My mom was OUTRAGED. I had never seen her freak out like that—before or since. My teacher Mr. Aufmann received a call from at least one angry parent that day. I didn't understand her reaction at the time, but I do now.

Planned Parenthood's motivation for "helping" women becomes clear—and disturbing—when you learn about the company's founder, Margaret Sanger. Sanger was a believer in eugenics, the idea of creating a superior society by encouraging procreation among the higher classes, and discouraging it among the poor and uneducated classes.[36] As a resident of New York City, Sanger first implemented her "Negro Project" by establishing a birth control clinic in Harlem, a predominantly black neighborhood, in 1923.[37] In short, Sanger sought to reduce or eliminate the black population through various birth control methods, including abortion.[38]

Even today, 62% of Planned Parenthood's abortion clinics are located in "targeted neighborhoods" where there is a high African American population.[39]

Sanger's influence on the African American community is tragic. Each year more African American children are aborted in New York City than are born.[40] Even abortion activist groups such as the Guttmacher Institute admit that black women are more than five times as likely as white women to have an abortion.[41]

New Life for the Pro-Life Movement

A new trend has recently started. After years of being championed by the Catholic Church and Evangelical believers, predominantly from suburban churches, there is new life for the pro-life movement. Joining the fight are influential, Conservative-Christian men from the black community who recognize that their population has suffered the most from Planned Parenthood's targeting of poor black neighborhoods.

In 2019, Kayne West declared his pro-life views in a radio interview promoting his new album *Jesus Is King.* West, the highest-paid rapper in 2019, admits that the black community has been "brainwashed" by progressive policies that advocated for them aborting their children.[42] His own father, he confessed, wanted him aborted.[43] This new stance represents a major swing for West who openly promoted abortion in his 2013 song "Blood on the Leaves" as a way to avoid consequences of extramarital affairs and the responsibility of fatherhood.[44] The new-and-improved Kanye 2.0 has breathed new life into an old debate.

Also joining the fight is David J. Harris, Jr., author of *Why I Couldn't Stay Silent: One Man's Battle as a Black Conservative.*[45] In the book, Harris shares his deeply rooted conviction about the right for life as a conservative, as a believer, and as a father. In fact, he feels so strongly about the pro-life, anti-abortion position that he asserts that it is the single most important issue when it comes to voting.[46]

Many from every ethnic and socioeconomic class are finally coming to understand that abortion is not healthcare; it's genocide—a coordinated and systematic killing of a racial or cultural group.

The Role of Rules

What about the argument that it is unconstitutional for the government to tell women what they can and cannot do with their bodies? This is considered the basis for the legal argument of *Roe v. Wade*.

Consider this: In a state where there are no restrictions on abortion—such as New York—a mother could legally abort her son or daughter the day before her due date. If, however, en route to the abortion clinic a driver strikes her car, killing her and her unborn child, the driver could be charged with *two* counts of vehicular manslaughter. The absurdity and irony of this hypocrisy in our legal system is breathtaking.

If a pregnant woman is legally considered to be two separate people, it stands to reason that her "rights to her own body" end where the next life begins.

For this reason, many states have begun adopting the Human Rights Protection Act, more commonly known as the *Heartbeat Bill*. This legislation bans abortion as soon as a fetal heartbeat can be detected, as early as six weeks into pregnancy. This bill allows for exceptions when the life of the mother is in jeopardy, but not for rape and incest cases. Under this law, doctors who violate these terms could incur criminal penalties.[47] As of this writing, Georgia, Kentucky,

Louisiana, Mississippi, and Missouri have passed this bill or one similar.

The government of any developed nation has both a right and responsibility to protect all citizens, especially those who cannot speak for themselves. The primary role of government is to restrain evil, according to John Eidsmoe, author of *God and Caesar: Biblical Faith and Political Action* (Wipf and Stock Publishers, 1997). The fight for life is not only constitutional, it is also the obligation of any citizen of the kingdom of heaven.

America is in a fight for her lives.

> Abortion isn't healthcare;
> it's genocide.

DISCUSSION GUIDE

Chapter 6: The Rights of Life

The purpose of this section is to help you facilitate a meaningful discussion surrounding the material in this chapter. Please refer to Appendix: Tips for Leading Small Group Discussions.

1. Can you summarize the main idea of this chapter?

2. What does the term "eugenics" mean?

3. Do you think the government has the right to place restrictions on abortion? Why or why not?

4. Many have said that abortion is the primary issue they use to determine which candidate to vote for. Do you agree or disagree? Make your case for why or why not.

5. According to John Eidsmoe, "The primary role of government is to restrain evil." Name some other areas or policy issues where this idea already is or should be applied.

6. How can we, collectively or individually, encourage adoption in our culture over abortion?

Scriptures to read and discuss:

• Psalm 139 (entire chapter)

• Proverbs 19:8

• Galatians 2:20

• Genesis 9:5–6

• Ephesians 5:15–16

• Proverbs 25:26

Family Matters

One of my heroes is my mother-in-law, Mary-Ann Travis. My husband Perry is the fourth of five sons in the Travis family. Mary-Ann had the unenviable task of raising five boys on her own after her husband left when the youngest son was a year old.

With little help from government assistance programs, Mary-Ann worked several jobs in order to feed her family and keep their home. The older sons needed to pitch in to the family finances, too. Perry recalls his older brothers handing over their paychecks from their high school jobs to mom to pay the bills. Christmas and birthdays were pretty lean, as you may imagine.

In spite of the immense challenges she faced, Mary-Ann was one of the kindest and most compassionate individuals I have ever met. She was quick to forgive, even those who hurt her deeply. If you knew her, you understood that—next to her sons—her faith in Jesus Christ was the most important thing in her life. And if you didn't know this, she would be sure to tell you. Mary-Ann would walk up to strangers in restaurants to talk about Jesus, and she would pray for the local plumber before she would let him conclude his service call.

Perry would call or visit his mom every Father's Day, in addition to the typical holidays. She had to be both mom and dad, a task that she took seriously. Mary-Ann took literally the promise in Psalm 68:5–6 that God was her husband.

> Father to the fatherless, defender of widows—
>   this is God, whose dwelling is holy.
> God places the lonely in families;
>   he sets the prisoners free and gives them joy.

Momma Travis went to be with Jesus on January 2, 2019. I will forever remember her kindness to me and her faithfulness to God.

Love and Marriage

The family is the earliest institution established. God created man in his image. He created the woman so man wouldn't have to be alone, and He gave them both the command to be fruitful and multiply. The Creator of the universe could have populated the earth any way He wanted, but He chose to create families.

God created the family for the purpose of protecting and preserving its participants. We understand how children benefit from the family unit, but the same is true for adults, too.

Both secular and faith-based studies on health and wellness conclude the same thing: marriage is beneficial to the individual. Consider a study from Harvard Medical School first published in 2010 and updated in 2019 that discusses married men and mortality. The survey of over 120,000 individuals found that married men are healthier than unmarried, widowed, or divorced men.[48]

The study also concluded that marriage has a positive effect on a variety of health outcomes, specifically mental health. Married men have a lower risk of depression, reduced risk of Alzheimer's disease, improved blood sugar levels, and a greater probability of recovering from serious physical conditions.[49]

Remarkably, the same or similar results were discovered in countries all over the world. In addition to the American study, Great Britain and Japan also recorded findings that marriage was positively linked to greater health outcomes.

Some of these studies went so far as to suggest that the quality of the marriage had little effect. Married men with poor relationships with their spouse still enjoyed greater health and happiness than their never married or divorced counterparts.

Other studies have concluded that marriage is a surprising predictor of wealth.[50] A study from the University of Michigan concluded that "getting married increases wealth and income."[51] Even those who disparage marriage, for one reason or another, have a difficult time explaining away this phenomenon.

If adults fare better within the family unit, it goes without saying that the benefit for children is even greater. Children in two-parent households are more likely to get As in school, enjoy school, and enroll in extracurricular activities. As teenagers, these children are less likely to abuse drugs, drop out of school, and have children outside of marriage.

> God created the family for the purpose of protecting and preserving its participants.

Orphans, on the other hand, have always been and always will be the most vulnerable population of any society.

In recent years, my family has enjoyed the pleasure of being involved with an orphanage in Kagadi, Uganda in East Africa. On our first trip to Uganda in 2018 we met Robert and Milly Kikomeko, a young couple who started a school/orphanage at their own expense to care for the growing number of vulnerable children in Robert's native village. Uganda has one of the highest orphan populations in the entire world—largely due to the AIDS epidemic in this region—with more than 12% of all children likely to end up on the streets or worse.[52]

Robert and Milly recognized that children who are compromised because of the absence of parents or a dysfunctional family situation are at much greater risk to be abandoned, abused, or trafficked—including the practice of childhood marriages, still common in rural Uganda. As a result of the compassion and dedication of this one couple, over four hundred and fifty children are cared for at Maisha School and Orphanage. We love Robert and Milly so much that we've unofficially adopted them into our own family.

Closer to Home

Here at home we face a different epidemic that threatens our society—the absence of fathers. The lack of a father in the home poses very serious risks to the health and wellbeing of a child.

Poverty is regarded as the greatest risk for families without a father at home. Women-only households are significantly more likely than two-parent households to live below the poverty line. Children from these families are vulnerable to many hardships, both economic and social, throughout their lives.[53]

Statistics from the U.S. Department of Health and Human Services, Bureau of the Census, and other government sites tell the following story:

- 63% of youth suicides are from fatherless homes

- 85% of children who show behavior disorders come from fatherless homes

- 90% of all homeless and runaway children come from fatherless homes

- 80% of those convicted of rape and other violent offenses come from fatherless homes

- 85% of all youth in prison are from fatherless homes

Special thanks to Sabrina, author of The Fatherless Generation Project for collecting these statistics from government websites.[54]

I would like to acknowledge that many, many adult children who grew up without fathers have overcome the challenges and live fruitful, productive lives. Many of these men, like my husband, develop a greater commitment to their children and families as a result of being abandoned by their own fathers. Some will tell you, however, that having male role models and mentors made all the difference in their lives. The brutal truth is that fathers, even more than mothers, have a direct and undeniable impact on their offspring.

Fatherhood Failures

Tragically, absent fathers and the problems associated with them have adversely affected the black community more than any other ethnic group in our country.

Jack Brewer, a former NFL player with the New York Giants, is also an evangelist who has initiated a prison ministry through his foundation. Brewer acknowledges that as many as 77% of babies born in the black community are born to single moms. "The number of kids that don't have fathers or positive male influences is devasting," according to Brewer. "Our institutionalized system has made this acceptable in black culture today."[55]

Brewer's foundation has implemented programs to teach business and leadership skills to incarcerated men. Brewer is committed to bridging the gap of missing fathers within the black community through improved legislation and rehabilitation. This course offered through the prison systems in Texas qualifies under the First Step Act[56] enacted under the Trump Administration to give reduced sentences to men who successfully complete the program.

"The program is about rehabilitation, but at the core, it's about fatherhood. We talk about not just the father in the flesh, but about our Father in heaven."[57]

Under Attack

Given the extraordinary, God-given protection offered to both adults and children, it's no wonder that the family structure and institution are under attack. God created the family to protect and preserve its participants. It only makes sense that Satan would seek to destroy the family.

In an early experiment with socialism in America in 1826, Robert Owen—originally from England—purchased property in Harmony, Indiana, and set up a colony which he said would produce morally superior human beings. Owen called the settlement "New Harmony."

Owen proclaimed the liberation of humankind would happen through the elimination of the "Trinity of Evils" responsible for all of humanity's misery: traditional religion, *conventional marriage*, and private property. Owen's prescription for paradise included abolishing the church, disrupting the family structure, and eliminating capitalism. His social experiment in America was a spectacular failure and he moved back to England.[58] We'll explore socialism in detail in Chapter 10.

Historically, any attempt to usurp the natural order of marriage and family leaves its members vulnerable and results in chaos.

China, for example, instituted its one-child policy in 1979 designed to systematically decrease the growing population of China. This policy imposed harsh consequences for families with multiple children, thereby encouraging parents to give up—and even kill—their daughters in order to have a son to carry on their family name. Families who defied the policy were punished with financial sanctions or worse. Many women were forced to have IUD insertions, abortions, and even sterilizations.[59]

This policy has had devastating consequences on the family structure in China. Families are experiencing the four-two-one problem. There are four grandparents and two parents who will look to a single child for care and financial support. Also, the intended and unintended consequences of this policy left China with significantly more males than females. Hundreds of single men of marriageable age are competing for one woman. Family life as we know it will be extinct in China within a matter of generations.

China is not the only country to experiment with the family structure. In the last ten years Cuba has become a haven for the LGBT community. This may seem like a victory for human rights, but it's not. Raul Castro supports homosexuality as a means of population control. Less babies being born will eventually lower the population on the island. In addition, encouraging the breakdown of the traditional family will isolate more individuals, thus strengthening the regime's hold on its citizens.

America is in the midst of its own social experiment seeking to disrupt and uproot the traditional family. The political organization Black Lives Matters (BLM) is masquerading as an advocate for minorities and under-served communities, but that's not their mission.

> Historically, any attempt to usurp the natural order of family and marriage leaves its members vulnerable and results in chaos.

BLM's intended mission is to "disrupt the Western-prescribed nuclear family structure requirement."[60] This objective is very different from what most Americans believe about the Black Lives Matters movement. Many in minority communities have jumped on the bandwagon believing that BLM is supporting them. But, rather than advocating for black families and communities, the group has a very different agenda.

It's shocking, actually, to see what this group is up to. According to their mission statement, BLM is intended to "make space for transgenders to lead, and to dismantle the patriarchal practice of mothers caring for their children so that they have time to protest for social justice." This sentence refers to transgenders taking a communal approach to raising children, so that the biological mother or father isn't tied down to parenting responsibilities and is free to join in protests. Their website states their true intention—namely, freeing themselves from the tight grip of "heteronormative thinking." We'll explore this more in Chapter 8.

The irony of their name can be seen in the destruction this group has caused in minority communities. BLM has undermined law and order by burning black-owned businesses and demanding the defunding of the police. It stands to reason that those who suffer most when police protection is taken away are vulnerable women and children.

The Wrap-Up

A wise man once said, "Family is the original Department of Health, Welfare, and Education."[61] God designed the family to protect and strengthen its participants—to protect us! Health, wealth, and companionship are some of the greatest advantages the family offers. Everyone within the family unit benefits both physically and emotionally when the family remains intact.

Thankfully, many brave individuals have learned to thrive, despite all of the challenges associated with divorce, abandonment, and the general breakdown of their families.

Fathers play a monumental role in the family structure. The absence of fathers can be directly tied to poverty, crime, and hopelessness for the women and children they leave behind. Men face enormous pressures and challenges in today's society which threaten their own livelihoods, as well.

Satan, the "father of lies,"[62] seeks to destroy the institution of the family. His plan is to leave men, women, and children exposed and vulnerable. He infiltrates societies, governments, and individuals to spread his lies and deception.

There is a beautiful, but haunting, promise in the book of Malachi. Verse 4:6 says, "[God's] preaching will turn the hearts of fathers to their children, and the hearts of children to their fathers. Otherwise I will come and strike the land with a curse."

This we know for certain—family matters!

DISCUSSION GUIDE

Chapter 7: Family Matters

The purpose of this section is to help you facilitate a meaningful discussion surrounding the material in this chapter. Please refer to Appendix: Tips for Leading Small Group Discussions.

1. Can you summarize the main idea of this chapter?

2. What was most surprising to you about the statistics regarding marriage and health?

3. Why do you think married men live longer, according to the statistics?

4. Consider the statement, "Family is the original Department of Health, Welfare, and Education." Can you give an example of how the family unit protects, provides care, or educates an adult or child?

5. Do you agree or disagree with the premise that the absence of fathers is a major problem in America? Provide examples to make your case.

6. How can we as individuals or collectively as the church help the "fatherless"?

Scriptures to explore:

- Deuteronomy 6:6–7

- Acts 16:31

- 1 Corinthians 1:10

- Proverbs 6:20

- 1 John 4:20

- Proverbs 3:11–12

Gender Reveal

I remember an incident that happened when my son Nick was in eighth grade. He was called to the principal's office after another student reported him for a comment he made. Nick was surprised by the summons, and not exactly sure what he did wrong. The assistant principal explained that another student was offended because he told her that *there were only two genders.* The school administrator then went on to inform him that the government just published a listing of over fifty-one genders (this was in 2016 during the Obama Administration), and that he has no right to challenge this.

Nick—being Nick—said, "No, there's only two genders. You can't convince me otherwise." Eventually the administrator let him off with a warning and told him that the next time he said this to another student he would be suspended.

I can tell you that this was a new one for us. I was a little disturbed by the administrator's remarks. But Nick assured me that he could handle it and because he wasn't suspended, there was no need for me to get involved. My only concern was that he acted respectfully toward the other student. I definitely wasn't upset that he told her there are only two genders.

For all of us that are over the age of fifteen who grew up thinking that there are only two genders, we have to wonder—what in the world is going on? Why, when for centuries, societies all over the world have endorsed the idea that there are only two categories in the gender column—male and female—are we being told that this is no longer the case?

A brief disclaimer at this point: I realize that there are abnormalities, and specific cases where babies have been born with both sets of sex organs, or neither. That happens in 1 out of 2,000 births, or .05% of the general population. Because we live in a fallen world, I'm not denying that it happens or that there are exceptions to the rule. But what I am addressing is the claim that the rules have changed.

The good news is that the biological facts have not changed: baby boys and baby girls continue to be born every day; the bad news is the way that we view these facts has changed.

In recent years there has been an effort to separate gender from biological sex. There is a belief in our current culture that sexual orientation is not dictated by the biological sex we were assigned at birth.

This belief by many is so firmly held that even the implication that men and women are different and distinct from each other—the natural order outlined in Genesis 1—is considered offensive. During the Supreme Court confirmation hearing of Amy Coney Barrett in October of 2020, Ms. Barrett drew criticism from the LGBTQ community by using the phrase "sexual preference" in response to a question from the Senate Judiciary Committee.

Senator Mazie Hirono, D-Hawaii, chastised Barrett for using the phrase because it suggests that sexual orientation is a choice. "Sexual orientation is a normal expression of human sexuality," Senator Hirono responded.[63]

Within days of this exchange, Merriam-Webster changed the definition of the term "sexual preference" in its on-line dictionary to include that it is considered "offensive" to suggest that a person can choose who they are sexually attracted to.[64]

Boys will be... Girls?

The idea that sex is different than gender is not only unsubstantiated, but also dangerous.

In an interview with Dr. Michelle Cretella, President of the American College of Pediatricians, she explained that "biological sex is not assigned, it is determined at conception by our DNA, stamped into every cell of our bodies. Human sexuality is binary. Either you have a Y chromosome and develop into a male, or you don't, and you will develop into a female. There are at least

6,500 genetic differences between men and women. Hormones and surgery cannot and do not change this."[65]

Dr. Cretella has received death threats from activists asserting her claim that biological sex as determined at conception is "hate speech."

Why, then, does there appear to be so much gray area if the facts haven't changed? We're seeing an entire cultural movement that no longer believes that an individual's biological composition dictates their gender.

Universities have developed entire degree programs around the study of theories surrounding human sexuality. There are words being disseminated throughout our culture that didn't exist ten years ago. When I conducted an internet search for the word GENDER, the following information appeared.

- Gender Studies
  Gender studies is a field for interdisciplinary study devoted to gender identity and gendered representation as central categories of analysis. This field includes women's studies, men's studies, and queer studies.

- Gender Dysphoria
  Gender dysphoria involves a conflict between a person›s physical or assigned gender and the gender with which he/she/they identify. People with gender dysphoria may be very uncomfortable with the gender they were assigned, sometimes described as being uncomfortable with their body (particularly developments during puberty) or being uncomfortable with the expected roles of their assigned gender.

- Gender Ambiguity
Gender ambiguity deals with having the freedom to choose, manipulate, and create a personal niche within any defined socially constructed code of conduct; while gender fluidity is outlawing all the rules of cultural gender assignment. It does not accept the prevalence of the two rigidly defined genders being "man" and "woman."[66]

I hesitated to print this chapter because I know my information will be outdated before the ink even dries on the page.

There is no consensus—even among those who deny that there are only two genders—on how many there really are. For example, when researching genders, I found articles claiming there were 33, 52, 58, and 64 different genders. In fact, one article entitled "Complete List of All Genders" listed forty-seven starting with the letter A![67] I've listed just a few to give you an idea:

- Affectugender – A gender affected by mood swings

- Agender – Having no gender or a lack of gender identity

- Ambonec – Identifying as both man and woman, yet neither at the same time

- Angenital – A desire to be without primary sexual characteristics, without necessarily being genderless[68]

As a believer in Jesus Christ, I am compelled to acknowledge the truth expressed in Genesis 1:26–27: God created humanity as male and female. The Bible is very clear on this and biology hasn't changed.

It's not an accident that God stated the obvious in the creation account. He knew in his infinite wisdom that a time was coming when the natural order which was established through creation would be challenged. If you look at what is happening in America, every single foundational truth is under scrutiny. Ideas widely accepted in every country and culture throughout history are now being brought into question. For example, it wasn't that long ago that marriage between a man and a woman was regarded as sacred, babies were born as boys or girls, and murder was punishable by law.

There's a "new normal" invading our society in post-postmodern America: no idea—regardless of how basic or simple—can be assumed as right, and every opinion is viewed as equal. What we are witnessing is the expression of a different worldview.

However, not all worldviews are created equal. There are consequences to disregarding natural order.

In 2010, President Barack Obama enacted the Affordable Care Act. This legislation redefined "sex" to include "gender identity" for the purposes of nondiscrimination.[69] This ruling had unintended outcomes. For example, a biological woman visited a hospital's ER complaining of abdominal pain. Because she identified as a man, doctors were required to medically treat her according to her gender identify rather than biological sex.

The woman, who didn't realize she was pregnant, ended up delivering a stillborn child as a result of the treatment she received.[70]

As an extension of this legislation, Obama later issued guidance to public schools to make all bathrooms and locker rooms transgender. If school districts disregarded this mandate, they could face a loss of federal funding.[71] This policy exposed students—primarily girls—to sexual abuse and exploitation.

In 2017, the Trump Administration reversed the Obama-era regulation that redefined "sex," citing it as unconstitutional and a violation of the 1993 Religious Freedom Restoration Act.[72]

Although former President Obama and others fought for transgender rights, the truth regarding these policies and protections is rising to the surface. John Hopkins University, the institution that pioneered gender-reassignment surgeries, abruptly halted this surgical procedure after a survey concluded that the sex-change surgery did not improve an individual's quality of life, and offered "no advantage in terms of social rehabilitation."[73]

Eventually the surgeries were resumed after pressure from the LGBTQ community, but Psychiatrist Paul McHugh, the hospital's chief of psychiatry for over twenty-five years, still believes that being transgender is a psychological, not biological problem.[74]

A disturbing article published in 2018 discussed how transgender patients at the Oregon Health and Science University complained that their sex-change surgeries were botched. Many of these patients suffered mutilation at the hands of the doctor. As the writer states, "The doctor basically used a bunch of transgender people to experiment on and gain experience without being properly trained."[75]

The tragic truth is that any attempt to override the natural order which God established at creation results in the weaker, vulnerable segments of a society being exploited by those more powerful. In the same way that unborn children—particularly minorities—are exploited by politicians who fear political backlash, so are confused, socially disenfranchised youth. They are being told that it's perfectly normal to be subjected to new, untested drug treatments and surgeries.

> So God created human beings in his own image. In the image of God he created them; male and female he created them.
>
> - Genesis 1:27

During an election town hall, Democratic presidential candidate Joe Biden suggested that children as young as eight-years-old should be allowed to decide if they want to become transgender. He added that there should be no discrimination against a child who makes this choice. "There is no reason to suggest that there should be any right denied your daughter… that your other daughter has a right to be and do."[76]

Biden's comments drew sharp criticism from observers on Twitter. One commenter replied, "Sure, because any parent who has sat there and listened to their kids change their minds on Halloween costumes 10 times in a month thinks this is a good idea."[77]

Another pointed example of how weaker individuals are being exploited by the stronger can be seen in how transgender females (individuals who have transitioned from male to female) are cleaning up in girls' sports. In February of 2019, transgender females competed—and won—the Girls' State Track Championship in Connecticut.[78] In fact, both first and second place were awarded to biological males competing as females. Connecticut is one of 17 states to allow transgender high school athletes to compete without restrictions.

Biology, not to mention common sense, tells us that males are physically stronger and are generally superior athletically to girls. Everyone understands this. When the US Women's Soccer team is looking for a competitive scrimmage leading up to the Olympics, they don't play the US Men's Team. Instead, they scrimmage a selected boy's high school team because they match up more competitively with the women's team. These talented women at the peak of their athletic careers understand that their male counterparts are naturally stronger and faster.

Allowing biological males to compete as girls against other girls could bring about the end of girls' sports.

Sex and Marriage

Individual governments can make laws acknowledging different unions—such as allowing same-sex marriage—but this doesn't change the natural order the Creator of the universe set in place.

The reason the Bible contains very strong warnings against ALL sexual sins, including promiscuity and extramarital affairs, is because these are regarded as committing crimes against our own body. God has assigned you ownership of your physical body and wants you to take care of it.

> Run from sexual sin! No other sin so clearly affects the body as this one does. For sexual immorality is a sin against your own body. Don't you realize that your body is the temple of the Holy Spirit, who lives in you and was given to you by God? You do not belong to yourself, for God bought you with a high price. So you must honor God with your body (1 Corinthians 6:18–20).

As the mastermind behind all of creation, God wrote the owner's guide for our life and existence on earth. Think of it as the manufacturer's instructions that you receive any time you purchase a car, appliance, or other product. Likewise, the Bible contains specific instructions on how to care for our physical bodies in order to receive the greatest return on our investment. The need for proper nutrition and exercise are also part of how God designed our bodies for maximum performance.

God created sex to be enjoyed and respected between one man and one woman in an exclusive, committed relationship within the boundaries of marriage. Any other sex acts are considered an abuse and can bring on consequences to our physical and emotional state. Sexually transmitted diseases, broken and/or abusive relationships, unwanted pregnancies, and even depression in certain cases could be considered some of the repercussions resulting from misuses of human sexuality.

Just as with any owner's guide, there is a strong warning against using a product in any manner other than originally intended. Doing so can void the manufacturer's warranty. In this case, coloring outside the lines when it comes to sex can jeopardize our ability to live healthy lives and enjoy fulfilling, long-lasting relationships. Heterosexual marriage relationships aren't always perfect by any stretch of the imagination. However, statistically speaking they last significantly longer and participants report higher levels of satisfaction than among homosexual partners.

The Wrap-Up

God created men and women distinctly and separate from each other at the beginning of time. Marriage between one man and one woman is one of the earliest institutions known to man and it has been recognized throughout history in every nation and every culture. This idea remains intact today. We can't gloss over the truth simply because the biblical viewpoint is unpopular and politically incorrect in our current culture.

Attempting to redefine sexuality is presumptuous and dangerous. This can lead to individuals becoming angry, confused, and exploited. In the words of conservative commentator, Tucker Carlson:

> Gender is not a social construct; it is a biological reality. Men and women are inherently different; they are not interchangeable. Pretending otherwise is not just absurd and anti-science it is also a sure-fire way to make healthy relationships impossible, families fail and a society collapse.[79]

Please understand—God does not hate gay people, transgenders, nor any other arbitrarily named group of individuals. Instead, God proves over and over again that He loves all individuals, for He created them in his own likeness. He goes to great lengths and personal pain to deliver and restore each one. The Creator of the universe and author of the human race doesn't judge us by the labels we wear, but by our motives, attitudes, and actions.

Likewise, our response as human beings, and especially as Christians, should be kindness and compassion. As discussed in Chapter 3 "The Truth About Love," we are all sinful, broken people. We can be tolerant and respectful of everyone, even when we don't agree with their choices.

What God is really saying when He says "no" is—don't do it, because this will hurt you. God—in his infinite wisdom—wants us to enjoy long-lasting, fulfilling relationships. He wants to protect us from unnecessary pain.

DISCUSSION GUIDE

Chapter 8: Gender Reveal

The purpose of this section is to help you facilitate a meaningful discussion surrounding the material in this chapter. Please refer to Appendix: Tips for Leading Small Group Discussions.

1. Can you summarize the main idea of this chapter?

2. What did Dr. Cretella, President of American College of Pediatricians, mean when she said "human sexuality is binary"?

3. If you are a parent, what concerns would you have with allowing—by law—a child as young as eight decide if they wanted to pursue a sex change?

4. Does your state allow biological males identifying as females to compete as girls in sports? Would you be for or against your state legalizing this policy?

5. What is our responsibility as Christians toward those who hold different views on human sexuality?

6. What should be our responsibility as Christians to get involved with policy decisions, such as the ones mentioned in this chapter, which could directly or indirectly impact future generations?

Scriptures to read and discuss:

- Matthew 19:4
- 1 Corinthians 6:9–10
- Ephesians 5:3
- Romans 1:26–27
- Colossians 1:27
- 1 Timothy 1:9–10

The Pursuit of Liberty

A merica. "The Land of the Free and the Home of the Brave."

You may recognize this as the last line in the Star-Spangled Banner written by Francis Scott Key as he watched a huge American flag raised by soldiers at Baltimore's Fort McHenry, after a critical victory over the British in 1814. This conflict, also referred to as the "Second War of Independence,"[80] was the first test of the new American republic.

The British had recently captured Washington D.C., burned the White House, and were now moving to invade Baltimore. They were confident that taking Baltimore—a thriving port city—would prove even more strategic than conquering the capital city. Major General Robert Ross, the commander of the British Army, felt certain that taking Baltimore would cripple the American war effort and provide a victory for England.[81]

With over ten thousand men and one hundred can-
nons, the Americans mounted a stronger defense than
anticipated. British warships were pressed to engage,
and they bombarded Fort McHenry with mortar fire.
However, because of the shallow waters surrounding the Port of Baltimore, the British fleet eventually
withdrew. The defeat of the British at Fort McHenry
in Baltimore was a decisive victory for the Americans
and led to both sides signing a peace agreement later
that same year.[82]

Unfortunately, many may not recognize that these
famous lyrics from the Star-Spangled Banner were
penned as a result of that fateful battle. In recent
years there's been a coordinated effort to erase history and reshape the narrative in our country. We are
seeing individuals disrespecting our flag, desecrating
our monuments, and erasing the brave heroes who
fought for our freedom.

During the summer of 2020, over 104 statues and
monuments commemorating our American history
were vandalized. Statues of Confederate and Union
soldiers alike have been toppled, defaced, or decap-
itated in Minnesota, Alabama, Florida, Georgia,
Illinois, New York, Oregon, Texas, Louisiana,
Virginia, California, and Washington, D.C. Although
these acts were committed under the guise of protesting our country's racist roots, many statues attacked
by vandals had nothing to do with slavery or racism,
such as the 120-year-old statue of an elk in Portland,
Oregon.[83]

Petitions are being filed with the U.S. House of Representatives to remove "under God" from the Pledge of Allegiance for all schools. Advocates of this view believe schools are forcing students to "believe in God" by allowing the phrase to remain in the pledge.[84] These individuals contend this verbiage violates their First Amendment rights.

The "Land of the Free" is facing unprecedented challenges that threaten our freedoms. Our heritage is being uprooted daily.

America's uniqueness lies in the fact that it is the only country expressly founded on the idea of religious freedom. The early settlers to America risked their lives and their children's lives to make the treacherous journey across the Atlantic Ocean in search of this elusive dream. It's highly unlikely that any of us in this country will experience the persecution and torture for our religious beliefs that those first Americans did back in England.

This persecution—including the seizing of land and assets and physical torture—came at the hands of the state-run church.

Now think about that for a minute. State-run church. We're not talking about the Methodist church of Pennsylvania. State-run churches, also known as state-sponsor religions, grant power to the government to tax, punish, torture, or kill you for not conforming to their laws. And let's be clear about this—state-run religions have absolutely nothing to do with God. State-run religion is a means of controlling the population.

In 1776, the United States of America declared independence from the oppressive, totalitarian British government, sparking the Revolutionary War. The men who signed this document understood the risk they were taking to secure their own freedom and the freedom of many generations to come. This heroic act didn't go without notice. England branded these men as traitors and hunted them down like animals. According to historian Allan Hicks,

> Five signers were captured by the British as traitors, and tortured before they died. Twelve had their homes ransacked and burned. Two lost their sons serving in the Revolutionary Army; another had two sons captured. Nine of the 56 fought and died from wounds or hardships of the Revolutionary War.[85]

In countries all around the world, government replaces God. There are no freedoms—religious, personal, or otherwise—because an individual has no rights. The government controls all the wealth, all the resources, all the land, all the people, all the time.

Consider nations where state-sponsored or state-run religions still exist: Afghanistan, Algeria, Egypt, Iran, Iraq, Jordan, Kuwait, Libya, Malaysia, Pakistan, Saudi Arabia, and Yemen, for example, have Islam as their state-sponsored religion. Also, in Cambodia, Sri Lanka, and Thailand, Buddhism is the state-sponsored religion. These countries are notorious for consistently and systematically violating human rights.

Unlike the horrific violations of basic human rights perpetuated by governments all over the world, the United States' Constitution grants us PERSONAL freedom. We have the ability to live where we want, pursue any career we want, and make as much money as we can. We can go to church anywhere we would like and practice any religion we choose.

This is why the Declaration of America's Independence from England was, and still is, so radical. No other nation on the face of the earth had ever granted such freedom to their citizens. The document signed by Congress on July 4, 1776 contains the following statement:

> We hold these truths to be self-evident, that all men are created equal, that they are endowed by their Creator with certain unalienable Rights, that among these are Life, Liberty and the pursuit of Happiness.

As difficult as it may be to comprehend, personal freedom—the right to own property, to build wealth, to protect yourself and your family, and to pursue happiness—didn't exist prior to 1776. The Founding Fathers who secured our independence from England were conducting a social experiment called America.

In 1787, four years after the newly formed American army defeated the British in the Revolutionary War, the Founding Fathers drafted the Constitution to establish rules for the novel government. These laws were based on the idea that God created the universe and thus is the only one who can give life and take it away—not the government. The creators of the

Constitution patterned the new form of governing after the ideals found in Scripture: freedom to worship, sacredness of human life, the ability to own private property, the traditional family, and free markets.

Freedom of religion was front-and-center when the Constitution was written. The founders understood the undeniable connection between religious freedom, capitalism, property rights, and prosperity.

Contrary to popular opinion, the notion of the separation of church and state isn't a liberal ideology, it references the First Amendment to the Constitution:

> Amendment I
>
> Congress shall make no law respecting an establishment of religion, or prohibiting the free exercise thereof; or abridging the freedom of speech, or of the press; or the right of the people peaceably to assemble, and to petition the government for a redress of grievances.

Previously, the church and state were the same thing. Government was intended to be sovereign—our provider, our security, and our savior. Separating the two entities in this new government system allowed the individual freedom to worship the Creator, not the government.

The amazing thing about our Constitution is that it guarantees freedom for all religions. Americans are free to practice their faith as Jews, Christians, Muslims, Buddhists, and the like, as long as it is done peacefully and within the boundaries of the law.

Governed by God

Fast-forward two hundred years. In post-post-modern America there is a notion that separation of church and state means that government and governing institutions should not be influenced by Christianity *in any way*. Advocates for this erroneous interpretation of the church-and-state debate have been slowly pecking away at the foundation of our Constitution, especially with respect to freedom of religion.

There is no factual or historical basis for the removal of Christianity from the Rule of Law in America. As mentioned above, our Constitution is built on the foundation of biblical Christianity. The brave young men who rebelled against the tyrannical government in England understood this truth.

William Penn, the colonist who purchased Pennsylvania said, "Men must be governed by God or they will be ruled by tyrants." Penn's hope for Pennsylvania was for it to become a refuge for Quakers and other persecuted people groups. He had a vision for building an ideal Christian commonwealth.[86]

Like many others, Penn understood that if we reject the protections offered through the natural order which God established at creation, we leave ourselves open to be exploited by power-hungry dictators and oppressors.

Make no mistake. It is *impossible* to separate Christianity from politics. Did you know that 37 of the 39 books of the Old Testament in the Bible were written to, about, or by political leaders? The historical books of the Old Testament outline the founding, establishment, and subsequent fall of the nation of Israel. We see kings, judges, tribal elders, and oppressive foreign governments mentioned throughout Scripture.

Moses established local governments to rule over the millions of Israelites in their temporary camps.

> [Moses] chose capable men from all over Israel and appointed them as leaders over the people. He put them in charge of groups of one thousand, one hundred, fifty, and ten. These men were always available to solve the people's common disputes. They brought the major cases to Moses, but they took care of the smaller matters themselves (Exodus 18:26-28).

Prophets in ancient days served as consultants to kings. They were political advisors! They were not men with long robes that stood at the entrance to the temple and chanted. And as we see with Jeremiah, Nathan, and Ezra, many of them had a seat at the table and the ability to direct both foreign and domestic policy. The prophet Nehemiah served on the cabinet for the Persian King Artaxerxes and eventually led a coalition of Jews to return to Israel after years of living in exile.

It's Not You, It's Me

Please don't be fooled. The fight to extrapolate Christianity from modern society isn't an innocent misunderstanding or the expression of another viewpoint, it's a coup attempt. America is under siege. The attempt to obscure Christianity in American government by some in leadership is part of a larger plan to "fundamentally transform America" by creating separation between modern America and the Constitution.

When disenfranchised young people, graduates of our state-run colleges and universities, began vandalizing and tearing down historic monuments and statues, they weren't protesting American's racist roots. If this were true, they wouldn't have toppled the statue of a Catholic priest and Abraham Lincoln, the man accredited with liberating the slaves.[87]

> America's uniqueness lies in the fact it is the only country expressly founded on the idea of religious freedom.

No, the rioters were protesting our *Christian* roots, not our racists roots.

Furthermore, it is important to understand that every government is guided by some type of belief system. Democracy is shaped by Christian principles. In contrast, Communism is guided by Marxism, and Sharia Law is directed by Islam.

Sharia Law, as observed in Saudi Arabia, Afghanistan, Iraq, and many other countries in Asia and Africa, extracts guidance from the Quran on penalties for behavior. For example, theft is punishable by amputation of the hands (Quran 5:38).[88]

Separation Anxiety

Many Americans are confused about the need for creating barriers between religious institutions and the government. These are the same individuals removing the Ten Commandments from walls of courtrooms. They reason that separating church and state means our legal system shouldn't be influenced by Christianity. But the separation of church and state was never about protecting the government from the church! Many in power today would like us to believe that, but it's simply not true.

The purpose of separating the church and state was *to protect individuals from the government, not the other way around.* Separation of church and state was always intended to guard our personal freedoms, not to protect the government from Christianity.

Perhaps the most disturbing finding is that historically, when a government deliberately rejects Judeo-Christian principles—such as capitalism and free markets, the sanctity of human life, and the ability of private citizens to own property—it does not bode well for that country's citizens. We'll discuss these principles more in upcoming chapters.

Just within the last one hundred years we've seen the rejection of these principles of governance in Germany, Cuba, Venezuela, and North Korea.

In 1960, one of the first things the rebel leaders did during the revolution in Cuba was to cut off the food supply, as a means of forcing submission.

Shortly after that, they destroyed churches and killed pastors because religion is viewed as an enemy of the state. The regime was confident that if they could indoctrinate the people—particularly the youth—Communism would take a firm hold in the hearts and minds of the Cuban people.

I was surprised to discover that even Germany was a democracy prior to 1933. Hitler and other Nazi leaders disrupted the democratic process by burning down the Reichstag, their parliamentary building, one week before the election was to take place.[89] Hitler capitalized on the chaos to seize power. Within the next forty-eight hours, he unlawfully imprisoned and tortured four thousand of his political enemies.[90]

German society, which previously valued human life, was soon replaced with Hitler's version of Darwinism. Evolutionary theory suggests that different races of people evolved at different times and rates, causing one race to be superior to another. And while some don't believe Darwin ever fully envisioned the consequences of this flawed line of thinking, many believe Adolf Hitler's obsession with racial purity and the demonization of the Jews was fueled by Darwin's conjecture.

We all know what happened soon after that with the ethnic cleansing campaign that began with the elimination of its most vulnerable populations: the sick, elderly, and children.

When Christianity and its governing principles are removed from government, individual rights and freedoms are often sacrificed in the process.

The Fall of Democracy

It's hard to imagine that our beautiful Democracy in America—built and paid for by the blood and sweat of the brave founders—could ever be destroyed. But history tells us otherwise.

Even the mighty Roman empire fell, the superpower that encompassed much of the known world for over five hundred years. Historians don't agree on the precise reasons, but most concur that political corruption and over-spending were significant reasons.

How exactly does a democracy fall? We have seen from history that three major factors contribute to the fall of a democratic society:

1. Deny religious freedom through fear and intimidation to create sole allegiance to the government.

2. Ruin the economy through extreme taxation, oppressive regulations, and replacing private enterprise with inefficient government oversight.

3. Allow bad-actors into government, thus increasing wide-spread corruption.

Simply put, any attempt to topple a democratic governing system is a play for power.

We should be very concerned when some in our government are attempting to remove our history, destroy capitalism, and "fundamentally change" our society. These attempts have nothing to do with social justice and have everything to do with ushering in a dictatorial power within government.

Major Amir Tsarfati, a decorated officer in the Israeli Army, said in a *Happening Now* event in Southern California, "Socialism always comes to power in a semi-democratic way but will never let go of power until there is bloodshed. I've seen it many times all over the world."[91]

The Wrap-Up

America was founded on the idea of religious freedom. But Democracy—government by the people and for the people—is under attack in America. Our freedom to worship our Creator in any way we choose is the primary cornerstone on which this country was built, but it is slowly eroding away.

Unfortunately, not all Americans recognize what is at stake here. The loss of freedom of religion is more tragic than we could imagine.

Worldwide, biblically based Christianity is the only religious system that supports personal freedom and is compatible with a democratic government. Attempts to remove Christian values by a government are a coordinated effort to suppress individual rights and usher in a dictatorship.

The separation of church and state is intended to protect citizens—to protect you and me—from unlawful interference by the government in private matters, including the freedom to worship. The government replaces God in systems such as socialism, Communism, Marxism, and others. When Christian principles are removed and a democratic system of government is replaced with socialism, it never goes well for that country's citizens.

I recently spoke with a friend whose family escaped from Cuba in the early 2000s. His words were very chilling. He said, "If America's great Democracy falls, there will be no place left to go."

If we allow our Constitution to be compromised and our Christian roots upended, we will suffer the fate of other failed countries—the very nations from which our citizens originally fled in pursuit of liberty.

DISCUSSION GUIDE

Chapter 9: The Pursuit of Liberty

The purpose of this section is to help you facilitate a meaningful discussion surrounding the material in this chapter. Please refer to Appendix: Tips for Leading Small Group Discussions.

1. Can you summarize the main idea of this chapter?

2. Consider this statement from the Declaration of Independence: "We hold these truths to be self-evident, that all men are created equal, that they are endowed by their Creator with certain unalienable Rights, that among these are Life, Liberty and the pursuit of Happiness." Do other countries uphold this standard? Have you been to countries who do not?

3. Discuss the idea of "separation of church and state." How do you interpret this statement? Do you agree or disagree with the author's interpretation?

4. Many Christians point to Romans 13 as a basis for respecting government authority. Do you think that applies all the time? What do you think would have happened if the men who fought for America's independence would have taken that position toward the British Government?

5. Do you agree or disagree with the statement: "It is impossible to separate Christianity from government?" Give examples of your position.

6. What do you think people mean when they say they want to fundamentally change America?

Scriptures to read and discuss:

- Romans 13:1–5
- 1 Timothy 2:1–2
- Galatians 5:1
- 1 Peter 2:16
- 1 Thessalonians 5:12
- Romans 13:7

A video on this subject entitled "Should Church and State be Separate" is available on the FUSION Leadership Group Site:
https://www.fusionleadership.site/toughquestionseries

Socialism Distancing

In February of 2015, we had the opportunity to visit Cuba. My husband and I spoke at a leadership conference to a group of over three hundred pastors in Santa Clara, central Cuba. It's a beautiful country with amazingly resilient people. We absolutely loved our time there but were heart-broken at the abject poverty we witnessed.

On our second day there, we visited a family who hosted a church in their home in a remote area. Since the government notoriously shuts down churches—often leveling them to the ground—Christians are forced to hold church in their homes. The church of this particular family consisted of ninety regular attenders on any Sunday morning. They met in their living room, an area approximately twelve-feet-by-twenty-feet!

This couple had three sons as well as another family member living with them, but I only noticed one bed—a dirty mattress sitting on the concrete floor.

Cubans are highly educated, hardworking people, even though each worker makes the equivalent of $30 per month. This is true regardless of profession. Custodians make the same amount as doctors in this country. They are not given a choice of where they go to college, or even which career they will pursue—the government tells them what they will study. Young men are forced to join the military, known as compulsory service.

The Castro brothers "sell" doctors, engineers, and other highly trained professionals to other countries to work in desolate, high crime areas where their local citizens refuse to work. The receiving country pays the Castros, not the employee or even the government. An individual can't refuse because if he does he will never work again since everyone works for the state.[92]

The citizens of Cuba do not have the ability to pursue happiness or liberty.

The socialist mantra is, "From each according to their ability, to each according to their needs." This sounds reasonable, doesn't it? Many dictators and autocrats rose to power by promising to build a utopian world where there is no struggle between economic classes, and everyone gets what they need. Karl Marx, author of the infamous *Communist Manifesto* believed that capitalism was doomed to fail, but abundance and harmony were achievable if communities would commit to sharing resources and denounce private ownership.[93]

Many across the world took the bait. At one point in the late 1970s, sixty percent of people worldwide were under socialist governments.

Social Experiments

There's a long list of failed experiments with socialism. The widespread devastation caused by World War II left many countries scrambling for new solutions. European colonialism—the practice of Great Britain and other wealthy countries exerting political and military authority over many smaller territories in order to exploit them for cheap labor and abundant natural resources—had failed. Countries previously controlled by Great Britain or other nations were finally establishing their independence.

Future leaders fighting to gain power across the world saw socialism—in one form or another—as a shortcut to economic prosperity for their struggling countries. If the government controlled all means of production, they reasoned, wealth could be redistributed evenly so that everyone would benefit. This proved to be an illusion in every case.

Some of these experiments began quite innocently. Julius Nyerere in Tanzania, East Africa, sincerely believed that he could rebuild the country and increase its wealth. But instead of creating economic prosperity through a market economy, Nyerere ordered all citizens to abandon their private property and move to collective farms where the government would redistribute the spoils. Instead of generating wealth, these policies proved to be very inefficient and led to more bureaucracy.

The people, now pushed to the brink of starvation, rebelled and burned down the villages.

Nyerere's flawed logic had tragic consequences: massive food and gasoline shortages. Government corruption exploded because it now held all the power. Instead of creating prosperity, his actions led to wide-scale starvation and despair.[94]

Other emerging leaders were not as naïve. Their promise to create a utopian society was nothing more than an elaborate and deliberate grab for power. Mao Zedong in China, for example, pledged his country-men the one thing they all wanted: life-long, basic economic security. The Chinese people soon came to realize the cost was submission. The Chinese govern-ment controlled everything in their lives, including who they married and how many children they had. Even the clothes they wore and the books they read were dictated by the government.[95]

Many brutal dictators successfully sold this dream of *peace on earth*, only to devastate their country's economy, oppress their people ruthlessly, and crush any opposition. Vladimir Lenin promised Russia "Peace, Bread, and Land" in 1918; Jawaharlal Nehru promised India the end of poverty in 1947; Mao Zedong promised China there would be open debate in 1956;[96] Fidel Castro promised Cuba prosperity in 1960; and Hugo Chávez promised Venezuela univer-sal healthcare in 1998.

Contrary to popular opinion, socialism and Communism are more similar than they are different, and socialism leads to Communism more often than it does not. Regardless of the intention or methods, one thing is clear from history: every single experiment with variations of socialism has resulted in epic failure and untold human suffering.

Venezuela was once Latin America's richest country and one of its longest-running democracies. Hugo Chávez rose to power by promising the poorest citizens of his country that the government would take care of them, provide free healthcare, and lift them out of poverty. His plan was to redistribute Venezuela's great wealth, primarily from its vast natural resources. The lower class believed him and he was overwhelmingly elected in 1998.

It appeared to work for a time—until oil prices plummeted. The government had abolished private industry and took over oil production. Under the new regime, production from oil refineries which had the capacity to produce 1.3 million barrels per day fell to 7,000 barrels per day. This was due to going years without maintenance and the breakdown of production systems.[97] Government can never run businesses as efficiently as private industry.

A university study in 2017 testified that Venezuelans reported losing an average of twenty-four pounds of body weight from starvation[98] in one year after their government oversaw the destruction of its democracy and economy, plunging much of the country into desperate poverty.[99]

Poverty, I've observed, is a political construct. Governments control the economic wellbeing of their citizens in the same way that a puppet master moves the strings on the marionette.

Democratic Socialism

This same promise of social utopia has been repackaged and sold in America as democratic social-ism. Alexandria Ocasio-Cortez, New York Congress-woman, promised single-payer healthcare, tuition-free public colleges, and a guaranteed living wage to all Americans in an interview with Business Insider in March of 2019.[100]

I feel like I've seen this movie before, and it doesn't end well.

Let's not forget that we already have a prototype of socialized medicine in the United States. It's called the VA. The Veterans Health Administration has the largest integrated health care system in the United States. Its 1,255 health care facilities, including 170 VA Medical Centers and 1,074 outpatient sites serve 9 million Veterans each year.[101]

The CBS hit drama *Seal Team* aired an episode in April of 2019 exposing the VA system. This episode, appropriately named "Medicate and Isolate," high-lights the struggle of a veteran by the name of Brett Swann who was seeking help for his war injuries.[102] Finally, after years of failing to hold down a job and losing every important relationship in his life, Brett recognizes that he suffered a traumatic brain injury during one of his many deployments.

He schedules another appointment at the VA, fully knowing what to expect. The show captures the long waiting lines, poor service, and hopelessness of many of the veterans waiting to be seen. After sitting in the waiting room for over eight hours, the receptionist tries to reschedule Brett's appointment—for over two months away! After being coerced by Brett's friend, the doctor eventually agrees to see him.

When Brett is finally seen, the doctor acknowledges that his symptoms definitely could have resulted from an explosion he encountered in Iraq ten years earlier. But since his injury went undiagnosed by doctors at the time of the event, the VA system rejects Brett for treatment for his brain injury. Instead, the overworked doctors and staff have no other option but to prescribe Brett with more anti-depressants.

The episode culminates when Brett—recognizing that he's out of options and hope—takes his own life in the parking lot of the VA facility. Yes, Brett is a fictional character and this is a drama series, not a documentary. However, CBS accurately captured the essence of the VA system and how it has failed some of our most faithful citizens.

The VA medical system developed after World War II granted power to the government to make healthcare decisions for our nation's Veterans. Although the system still works in many cases because of the dedicated medical professionals the government employs, the VA system has suffered several black eyes in recent years.

In 2014, a scandal involving then President Obama's mishandling of Veterans Affairs came to light. A Newsmax article disclosed how 35 veterans that year died while waiting for appointments to be seen at VA medical facilities, just in the Phoenix area. Across the country, at least another 24 veterans have died while waiting for care.[103]

Although still not perfect, the VA has turned the corner. The MISSION Act, under President Trump, took effect in June of 2019 and privatizes some care. This policy serves to give control back to Veterans to make decisions over their own healthcare.

Europe and Socialism

Many have claimed that socialism is working in Europe; however, this depends on your definition of success. There is a lot of confusion among Americans—understandably—concerning European politics.

Democratic socialists typically cite Sweden, the Nordic country in Northern Europe, as the example of where socialized medicine is successfully practiced. Sweden has a robust market economy predominantly comprised of privately-owned businesses which fund their vast social programs.[104] Sweden has also benefited from staying out of World War II and other global conflicts which would have depleted their national reserves.

In other words, capitalism funds Sweden's socialized healthcare system and other government-run programs. The government can finance these programs because the average Swede is taxed at a rate of nearly 50%.

Even though Sweden benefited initially from social-ized medicine, the healthcare system has fallen behind in recent years. According to Stanley Feld M.D., FACP, MACE, "Swedes are losing interest in the concept of a socialist society. The complaint is that it is inefficient, and, in most areas, the socialistic system does not work to the benefit of the people."[105]

> Poverty is a political construct.

For example, the town of Solleftea in Northern Sweden has 20,000 residents. The only maternity ward in town was shut down in 2014 to save the government money. Since the closest maternity ward is now over 125 miles away from town, midwives offer classes on how to deliver babies in cars—a skill which has proven very useful in many instances.[106] In an article in a local paper entitled, "Sweden's Health-care is an Embarrassment," author Johan Hjertqvist reports that waiting times in Sweden's hospitals are among the worst in Europe.[107]

The healthcare dilemma in Sweden has been exasperated in recent years by their immigration crisis. This crisis began in 2015 when over 100,000 refugees poured into the country from Syria,

Afghanistan and Iraq in just one year's time seeking asylum. An additional 70,000 refugees applied for asylum in the following two years.[108]

Swedes are very angry about the flood of immigrants pouring into their country and putting a strain on the healthcare system, delaying wait times for regular citizens.[109] To make matters worse, Sweden's over-extended healthcare system is one of the most expensive systems in all of Europe. Despite the scarcity of hospital beds, long wait times, and shortage of doctors and nurses, Sweden spends 11% of its GDP on healthcare.[110]

The welfare state created by liberal immigration policies is creating an unsustainable financial crisis in Sweden. The country of 9 million citizens—slightly larger than the population of New York City—has now committed to providing care to hundreds of thousands of refugees for life. The citizens of Sweden fear the long-term political, cultural, and economic effects to their country that only time will tell.

Other countries in Europe are not faring much better. In 2013, I had the opportunity to visit Brussels, Belgium to work with an international organization aiding victims of human trafficking. Two observations I made regarding Belgians from that visit: 1) it seemed that everyone drove a black BMW sedan, and 2) although many were helpful, very few Belgians ever smiled. One of the missionaries we worked with explained that even though Belgians have everything they need to live comfortably, most are unhappy.

The Belgium government taxes incomes at 51%, we were told. Business owners aren't concerned with providing good customer service, because it won't increase their profit margin. Belgians, according to my friend, are just going through the motions because they know they can never get ahead.

Recently the people of Great Britain issued a referendum on socialism by voting in Conservative Party leader Boris Johnson in 2019. Johnson won a decisive victory by securing 43% more of the popular vote than his rival; the largest winning margin in 60 years. Johnson's opponent, the leader of the Labour Party, Jeremy Corbyn, identifies himself as a democratic socialist. The people of Great Britain rejected the radical socialist ideology when they went to the polling booths that year.[111]

As Margaret Thatcher—the Prime Minister of England and the Conservative Party leader who rescued her country's economy in 1979 after years of failed socialist policies—said, "The trouble with socialism is that you eventually run out of other people's money."[112]

The Bible and Economics

What does the Bible say about the idea of "from each according to their ability, to each according to their needs," as the socialism mantra states? Scripture tells us more than you may think.

The very nature of mankind opposes the notion that we will ever have utopia here on earth. For socialism to work properly, benevolence and serving others instead of ourselves would have to be paramount. But people are selfish by nature. Paul spends a lot of time in his letters to the churches talking about our self-centeredness as human beings and speaking to the fallout this caused in the early Christian church.

At one point, Paul addresses a problem happening in the church at Thessalonica, a city located in modern day Greece. The year was circa 51 A.D. Certain individuals had become lazy and stopped working. They depended on others in the church for support. Instead of working to provide for their own food and necessities, these people felt it was the responsibility of the church.

Paul's response? "Those unwilling to work will not get to eat."[113]

Paul wasn't trying to be cruel; he was aiming to help all members of the church thrive by being self-sufficient. He understood how devastating it could be to an organization if a few individuals carried the responsibility for many others, especially those capable of providing for themselves. He also knew that this would free up valuable resources for those who were truly in need.

If we look back even further, we see basic social and economic principles in action in very early civilizations. Abraham, the man credited with being the "father of many nations," was very wealthy: he owned property, planted crops, hired workers, accumulated possessions, and protected his assets.

It's important for us to understand that every civilized society establishes rules to protect individuals and their ability to provide for themselves and their families. Throughout history, cultures that failed on this task didn't survive.

For example, the nation of Israel exists today because its founders understood these basic principles, even thousands of years ago. After the Jews' famous escape from Egypt, recorded in the book of Exodus, Moses is tasked with establishing a new, sovereign nation. The remainder of Exodus, Leviticus, Numbers, and Deuteronomy record God's laws and instructions for this brand-new society. These books record detailed instructions, among other things, on how to build buildings, plant vineyards, and prepare supplies they will need for survival.

The Ten Commandments given to Moses on Mount Sinai outlined the rule of law for this new nation and provided a basis for all civilized societies. Worship God first and only. Respect God's name. Honor your parents who gave you life. Don't murder. Don't sleep with someone else's spouse. Don't steal. Don't lie. Don't crave your neighbor's stuff.

These commands exemplify God's natural order. When properly applied, these rules can and have benefited every individual and society known to man since the beginning of time. When these laws are disregarded, however—such as "don't murder"—the results are devastating.

The idea of socialism is unnatural. From the beginning of time, individuals have benefited from hard work, self-discipline, and honesty. They have understood the need to provide for themselves and to protect their property and possessions from those looking for the "easy way out." It's not natural to work really hard so that the profit you make can be given to others who are lazy and do nothing.

This doesn't mean, however, that we shouldn't help others. We are compelled as citizens of heaven to help orphans and widows (James 1:27), care for the poor (Proverbs 19:17), and help strangers (1 John 3:17). But, according to the Bible, this is our individual choice and we'll be rewarded for our good deeds by God.

Charlie Kirk, founder of Turning Point USA, a non-profit organization advocating for conservative principles on university campuses, was asked if Jesus was a socialist. Kirk points out that Jesus was, first and foremost, the Savior of the world—not a political activist.

Kirk also points out that our charge as Christians "starts and ends with the individual calling, not the collective calling."[114] We can't abdicate our responsibility for providing for the poor or others in need to the government or anyone else.

We'll discuss this in more detail in the next chapter, *Capital Gains*.

The Wrap-Up

Socialism always begins with the promise of utopia but leads to tyrannical rule.[115]

Even prosperous democracies such as Germany in the 1930s, Venezuela in the 1990s, and Sweden in the 2010s, can succumb to destructive policies and mismanagement which bankrupt the economy and destroy the culture.

The failure of socialism is predictable because it defies the laws of nature. People are instinctively self-ish. And even though we are social beings and desire community, we all have an innate (natural) need for autonomy.

The erroneous idea that the government should own all property and distribute to all individuals evenly is an insult to our God-given intellect. To be candid, individuals never benefit from government control over the means of production or service providers, only the politicians in power.

"If socialists understood economics, they wouldn't be socialists," claimed Friedrich Von Hayek, the Nobel Prize winner in Economics in 1974.[116]

DISCUSSION GUIDE

Chapter 10: Socialism Distancing

The purpose of this section is to help you facilitate a meaningful discussion surrounding the material in this chapter. Please refer to Appendix: Tips for Leading Small Group Discussions.

1. Can you summarize the main idea of this chapter?

2. What is promised by democratic socialists in America?

3. Do you agree or disagree with the author's assertion that the Veterans Administration is a form of socialized medicine? Does this make you more confident or less confident in socialized medicine?

4. In what ways does the government seek to become "god" in our lives under socialism?

5. Do you agree or disagree with the author's claim that socialism (i.e., the government should collect and redistribute wealth) is unnatural?

6. Who do you think should be responsible for taking care of the poor?

Scriptures to read and discuss:

- Proverbs 10:22

- Proverbs 12:24

- Proverbs 13:11

- Ecclesiastes 5:18

- Hebrews 6:10

Capital Gains

Pastor Chris Griffin, a long-time family friend, told me about his trip to Uzbekistan in November of 2019. Chris was part of a delegation sent by the US State Department to the predominantly Muslim country in Central Asia.

"You went *where*?" I'm not sure that I had even heard of Uzbekistan prior to that day.

Chris explained the purpose for his trip to this relatively obscure country. A new leader rose to power in Uzbekistan in 2016 after 25 years of Communist rule. The newly appointed Prime Minister, Shavkat Mirziyoyev made a bold decision to move his country toward democracy by abolishing child labor, creating tax reform, establishing free trade, and offering amnesty to some political prisoners.[117] This verdict took many by surprise, including his own countrymen.

No one from the United States suspected the sudden move away from Communism toward democracy either. The Clinton Administration had designated Uzbekistan as a CPC or Country of Particular Concern in 1998 because of their flagrant human rights violations.[118]

Mirziyoyev, however, wanted to chart a fresh course for the Uzbeki people and enlisted the help of the US government. He and his administration invited this diverse group of ministers and lawyers from the United States to attend a forum focusing on religious liberty and increasing personal freedoms. This new Prime Minister took seriously his commitment to increase human rights and allow diversity of thought and religious expression by showing his commitment to changing the laws.

The country's strategic placement in the region showed great potential for commerce, and the new leadership wanted to capitalize on this. While he was there, Chris noticed some glimmers of hope—new construction projects and nice hotels—but he also noticed a lot of baggage left over from years of communist rule. Despite the prime minister's commitment to improving human rights, Uzbekistan still has over one million modern slaves trapped in the cotton industry, mostly women and children. This is over 4% of the country's population. Also, homosexuality is still illegal there and offenders could be fined or sent to prison.

Remarkably, with the enormous challenges the nation still faced, the quest for religious freedom was at the top of their list! The predominantly Sunni Muslim country technically allowed other religions to co-exist, but never encouraged it. They commonly used legislative means, such as making the application process cumbersome, to discourage diversity. Uzbeki leadership demonstrated their commitment to progress by streamlining the application process and enabling religious organizations to purchase their own property.

Senator Safoev, first Deputy Chairman of the Senate, made this amazing declaration during one of the meetings with the US delegation, *"You must have free hearts to have free minds, and you must have free minds to have free markets."* The new administration recognized the inexplicable connection between religious freedom, property rights, capitalism, and prosperity.

In August of 2020, Chris received word that the very first Evangelical Church in Uzbekistan officially made it on the books after their paperwork was approved.[119]

Capitalism has created more wealth and opportunity worldwide than any other economic system throughout history. According to Brett Bair in his video series "The Unauthorized History of Socialism," capitalism has been responsible for lifting over a billion people out of poverty.[120]

The United States of America—under capitalism—has held the reputation of the largest economy in the world since 1871. The United States holds a 23.6% share (nearly a fourth) of the world's economy with an annual Gross Domestic Product (GDP) of $21.44 trillion. The bottom 173 countries combined comprise less than one-fourth of the total global economy.[121]

An individual who makes just $34,000 annual income is in the top 1% of the richest people in the world, and half of the world's wealthiest individuals live in the United States![122]

Often citizens of other countries have the notion that ALL Americans are wealthy. Many developing countries welcome American tourists; some even beg for them to come to their country. I can personally attest to this truth, having traveled to Uganda, Rwanda, Cuba, and the Dominican Republic.

Our kids would concur with this, too. Our older two children have deployed to Kuwait, Afghanistan, Guam, and Qatar at various times while enlisted in the Air Force, and our youngest visited Myanmar with his youth group. They have visited some of the poorest regions in the world. Even in countries that have leadership that hate us, everyone wants what Americans have. It seems they know that—more than any other country—Americans are willing to share their wealth.

According to a MarketWatch article, "The United States is the No. 1 most generous country in the world for the last decade."[123] Americans are some of the most charitable individuals in the world, giving more than $427 billion in 2018 to US charities alone, to say nothing of charities worldwide providing relief to children and adults of impoverished countries. It's possible that this number is actually much higher since many have stopped claiming tax deductions for their charitable donations after the 2017 tax overhaul.[124]

Three reasons pointing to why capitalism is the superior economic system include: incentive, innovation, and competition, according to Mike Huckabee in his book *The Three C's That Made America Great* (p. 123). We'll explore these below.

Incentive: Unlike socialism, Communism, and other similar systems, capitalism rewards individuals for hard work. Other systems create dependence and penalize motivation. Without the motivation to improve, individuals, companies, teams, and even governments can become complacent.

My first experience coaching soccer came in my late 20s when I was the assistant coach for a boys' middle school team. In soccer, only 11 players are on the field at the same time and we had a roster of 33 players! This is every coach's nightmare. The team wasn't very good and I soon came to understand why.

The head coach's philosophy was that everyone got equal playing time. The players loved the idea that everyone had the same chance to play—at first.

Every game, regardless of our competition, resulted in a similar outcome. We would be competitive for the first 20 minutes, until the substitutions began. He would take out our top guys and sub in less skilled players. By the third round of substitutions, we had people on the field who had never played soccer before. They only joined the team to get out of their 8th period classes. We lost every game that year.

Halfway through the season Ben, our star player—the only one who could score—quit the team. He felt it made more sense to focus his energy on his Olympic Development team. With our team, he was not rewarded with more playing time for his skill or effort. Instead, the weakest players on the team were incentivized to stay without any expectations from them.

The next year I got my own team and never used that system again. The players who had invested the most time and intensity in developing their skills and getting in shape received the most playing time. Everyone had an opportunity to play but had to first prove their commitment to help the team.

Innovation: Capitalism rewards innovation, but socialism suppresses it. During the 2020 economic shutdown resulting from the COVID-19 pandemic, for example, innovation proved to be king. There was still profit to be made, but companies and individuals had to show ingenuity in order to overcome the drastic economic downturn due to restrictions.

Restaurants and the service industry were hit particularly hard during this time. Many closed their doors permanently. Others, however, thrived under the adversity. Sebastian Oveysi, Iranian-born chef and co-owner of Amoo's in Washington, DC, devised another plan when sales plummeted 65 percent at the beginning of the pandemic.

"Our family survived a revolution and the extremism that followed it. Then we escaped through a border covered in mines," said Oveysi. "We can get through a pandemic, too."[125] The business purchased a food truck and posted the truck's adventures on social media. Homeowners associations throughout the area took notice and now he has bookings every week.

Necker's Toyland, a toy store in Simsbury, Connecticut, that's been in business since 1948, also had to get creative. Sales at their retail stores tanked during the lockdowns, for obvious reasons. They began offering a FaceTime browsing option, virtually walking kids around the store, so they can pick out something that would keep them busy during the quarantine.[126]

Competition: Competition is a key reason why capitalism works. Competition forces down prices and creates accountability. When there is no competition—as in the case of major retailer Amazon and electronics lynchpin Apple—consumers lose their ability to control the market. Instead, the companies are in charge: they can hike prices, be careless with quality, and buy out prospective competition.

Competition benefits everyone. Competing companies benefit from increased marketing which exponentially expands consumer exposure. Bottled water is a prime example of an industry benefiting from product awareness. Even though the company Poland Spring began selling bottled water to summer visitors of their Maine resort in 1845, and Perrier mineral water began advertising in popular American magazines in 1910,[127] it wasn't until later in the twentieth century that bottled water became relevant. In the 1990s various US companies such as Deer Park, Nestle Pure Life, Arrowhead, Niagara, Smartwater, and others began producing bottled water, creating more attention and demand for the product.

The main reason many government agencies are notorious for poor service is because of the lack of competition. The Disney movie *Zootopia* released in 2015 comically portrays this stereotype. Judy Hopps, the bunny cop trying to solve a case, is delayed when she needs assistance at the Department of Motor Vehicles. Much to her dismay, all the employees at the DMV are sloths! (Sloths are the notoriously slow-moving mammals from South America who have become synonymous with the idea of being idle and lazy.) Needless to say, service at the DMV was extremely slow that day.

The school system in America has also fallen into this trap. The lack of competition in public schools has produced disastrous results, particularly in low income areas. According to the 2019 Nation's Report Card, only slightly more than one-third of eighth graders are proficient in reading.[128] The high spot of the report is that forty percent of fourth graders are proficient in math. Sadly, the good news equates to less than half of all ten-year-olds having advanced math skills.

Some areas of the country scored worse than others. Within the Baltimore City Public Schools, only thirteen percent of fourth graders tested above proficiency in reading.[129] Another alarming statistic points to the fact that nine-out-of-ten black boys in Baltimore City can't read at their current grade level. That means that in this region 90% of black men grow up without basic reading skills. Also, in over a dozen high schools across the district, not a single student tested proficient in math.[130]

To be clear, I have great respect for teachers. I personally know many, many exceptional professionals in this field. The problem isn't our teachers, it's the bureaucracy which eliminates competition and breeds complacency, particularly in minority neighborhoods.

For this reason, the Trump Administration and many of its supporters have declared School Choice—the ability of parents to use their own tax dollars to send their children to the school of their choosing—the Civil Rights issue of our time. Kim Klacik, the Republican candidate for Maryland's 7th District, ran her campaign based on the platform of how school choice seeks to break the "school-to-prison-pipeline" fueled by tragically ineffective schools in many inner cities.[131]

Proponents of school choice are confident this policy would force underperforming schools to improve by introducing competition within the public school system. When multiple schools are competing for the same students, schools will need to improve methods and results in order to stay viable.

The Downside of Capitalism

If you were to ask ten people the downside of capitalism, most likely nine of them would say greed.

It's true; there are many greedy people in our capitalistic society. Wealthy hedge-fund investors on Wall Street come to mind. Bernie Madoff, former chairman of the NASDAQ (National Association of Securities Dealers Automated Quotations) stock market became notorious for operating the largest Ponzi scheme in history. A Ponzi scheme is an elaborate financial scam where early investors are repaid with money received from later investors, not actual investment income.[132]

Madoff exploited his relationships with wealthy businessmen in New York and Florida in order to attract more investors. When he paid out handsome dividends (by using other people's money), these influential individuals encouraged their friends to invest with him, also. Madoff was indicted in 2009 when he plead guilty to fraud, money laundering, and other crimes. He is still serving his sentence in federal prison.

To say that capitalism is fueled by greed, however, is not substantiated.

Jay W. Richards dispels this myth in his book, *Money, Greed and God* (HarperOne, 2009). There is a difference between selfishness and self-interest, according to Richards. Capitalism is driven by self-interest because it seeks mutually beneficial transactions. For example, if you are a real estate agent you look to sell to people who need what you're offering—a home. Free markets exist because some have needs and others have products/services to fulfill those needs. Looking out for our self-interests isn't selfish, it's necessary for survival.

There's plenty of room for corruption in any economic system, whether it be socialism, capitalism, or any variation in between. The difference lies in who controls the power.

In capitalism, for example, the consumer is in control. Individuals have the option of choosing the car they will purchase, the house they will buy, the college they will attend, and the amount of savings they will invest. Unfortunately, unsuspecting consumers can be exploited by greedy, unscrupulous actors into investing in products or services which yield less than optimal returns.

Everywhere you look, powerful corporations are inventing ways to manipulate the customer. Advertisers invest millions to persuade and even coerce us. Most of us have been caught up at one time or another—and to one degree or another—by their deceptive plots. But, at the end of the day, the consumer is still in charge.

In socialism, however, the government is in power. Those who hold political power make all the decisions, as we discussed last chapter. This is why socialized medicine is not the answer. Yes, you may not have to pay for your doctor's visits, but a government bureaucrat decides which doctor you will see, when you will see them, what procedures you are authorized to have, and which doctor will operate. You may not get a bill in the mail, but you have lost control over your own care.

Capitalism isn't perfect, but it's worlds better than any other economic system.

Wealth and Poverty

The idea that capitalism contributes to poverty is another myth. Compelling evidence proves that the opposite is true.

The country of Venezuela was once a thriving democracy, as discussed in Chapter 10. In 1989, it's estimated that only 25% of households in the country were living below the poverty line. In 2017, however—after the deployment of socialistic policies designed to redistribute wealth took effect—87% of households were reported to be living in poverty.

There are a few reasons why countries with thriving market economies—where capitalism is at work—have fewer citizens below the poverty line than countries where the government controls all means of production. The first reason why the poorest individuals in a society do better under a thriving economy can be explained using "Reagonomics." President Ronald Reagan, when outlining his plan for the Economic Recovery Tax Act of 1981,[133] demonstrated how all members of society benefit from economic growth because those with the greatest resources can create the greatest opportunities. Prospects for employment at all levels of the salary scale improve under a healthy economy.

In a speech given in 1963, President John F. Kennedy explained the idea that general prosperity benefits the welfare of the individual this way: "As they saw on my own Cape Cod, a rising tide lifts all the boats."[134]

The second reason why an individual benefits in a society where the wealthiest members are prospering is the fact that those who benefit the most from capitalism tend to be the most generous.[135] As noted earlier in this chapter, America is the most charitable nation year after year. It's a widely accepted truth that Christian churches in America, and their members, have done more for the poor and underserved than any other group in the world. Soup kitchens, food pantries, homeless shelters, after school programs, playgrounds and recreation centers, services to train and integrate intellectually challenged youth and adults represent just a few of the benefits private, nonprofit groups provide here in the United States.

Capitalists aren't opposed to the redistribution of wealth. We just want to distribute our own fortune. We know that we are much more efficient at it than the government.

According to Jim Garlow in his book *Well Versed*, "Care for the poor is so close to the heart of God that He placed the role with the people of God. Apparently, He knew the government could not handle it properly."

The Bible and Economics (Part II)

In the last chapter we discussed the economics of the natural order God set in place at creation. From the beginning of time we see individuals working with their hands to plant crops, raise livestock, and sew clothes. They hired workers and protected their assets. The very fact that one of the Ten Commandments is "Do not steal" assumes that individuals own things. If the Israelite community was communal (they shared possessions) there would be no need to outlaw theft, because no one would have personal rights to any-thing.

Socialism always fails because it is not natural. It goes against the God-given desire to work and be productive in order to provide for yourself and family. Additionally, socialism doesn't align with our innate desire for autonomy.

In this era of participation trophies and entitle-ment, the Parable of the Talents found in Matthew 25 doesn't seem to make much sense to us. Many are perplexed by the idea that the man in the story doesn't treat everyone "equally." Allow me to summa-rize the story...

A business owner calls together his employees for a meeting. He's going out of town, so he puts differ-ent individuals in charge of his assets. He makes this determination based on each individual's ability: his star employee receives five talents, his two deputy assistants receive two talents each, and his under-performing worker only received one talent.

The first employee invests his boss' money and quickly doubles his savings from five to ten talents. The second and third employees also double their investments, ending with four talents each. The third employee was just plain lazy. Instead of investing and earning minimal interest, he hid the money and sat on it.

When the man returns to check on his assets, he finds a mixed bag of results. He's very pleased with the first three employees because they doubled profits on the money entrusted to them. But he's disappointed with the last employee—to say the least—because he didn't do anything with the one talent he had.

What happens next is most perplexing. He takes the one talent from the last employee and gives it to the *first*. If one of us were writing the story, we would probably have the business owner give two of the first employee's talents to the last guy to make things fair. Not only that, but the business owner severely chastises the last employee. In fact, the punishment is so harsh that it doesn't seem to fit the crime.

This story explains how God's economy is built on the foundation of rewarding hard work and obedience [to God]. We are given talents to use to glorify God, but these gifts also serve a practical purpose: they allow us to provide for ourselves and our families. Some are naturally gifted teachers, some are talented to work in the hospitality industry, others are skilled in the trades, many are natural "protectors" and work in public service, and others are skilled entrepreneurs.

We all possess God-given talents, and there are real consequences for refusing to work in ways God has gifted us.

Capitalism *is* the natural order God set in place at creation.

The Wrap-Up

Countries all over the world with thriving economies understand the connection between religious freedom, capitalism, and prosperity. Since 1970, capitalism has lifted over a billion people out of poverty.

Americans are some of the most generous in the world. The average American Christian, in particular, has volunteered their time and donated money to any number of charities, both here and overseas. Capitalists aren't against redistributing wealth, but we want the final say in how our money is used.

Free markets benefit *everyone*, including the poorest segment of the population. It's a misnomer that capitalism increases poverty. Instead of creating more poverty, capitalism creates more prosperity at all socioeconomic levels. Citizens of countries all over the world have risen out of poverty when their governments adopt policies that promote capitalism.

Deuteronomy 8:18 (ESV) says, "You shall remember the Lord your God, for it is he who gives you power to get wealth, that he may confirm his covenant that he swore to your fathers, as it is this day."

God, in his sovereignty, wants us to understand how to access the greatest capital gains.

DISCUSSION GUIDE

Chapter 11: Capital Gains

The purpose of this section is to help you facilitate a meaningful discussion surrounding the material in this chapter. Please refer to Appendix: Tips for Leading Small Group Discussions.

1. Can you summarize the main idea of this chapter?

2. Why do you think there is a connect between religious prosperity, property rights, capitalism, and prosperity?

3. Explain in your own words why competition is so important to capitalism?

4. Do you agree or disagree with the statement that "consumers have the final authority in capitalism"? Explain your position.

5. Why do you think the owner in the parable of the talents punished the third servant (or employee) so harshly?

6. Do you agree or disagree that capitalism is the economic system that God established for mankind? Explain your position.

Scriptures to read and discuss:

- Proverbs 13:11

- 1 Timothy 6:17–19

- Matthew 6:19–21

- Deuteronomy 8:18

- Philippians 4:19

- Proverbs 24:8–9

Capitalists aren't opposed to the
redistribution of wealth;
we just want to distribute
our own fortune.

After all, we are more efficient
at it than the government.

Race is On

2020—The year that went through the cheese shredder.

Like many, I distinctly remember December 31, 2019. No one had any idea of the oppression, despair, and isolation that would fall on us like a heavy coat just weeks later. A global pandemic of the COVID-19 virus originated in Wuhan, China and was subsequently exported to all of the known world. Just like that, everything changed.

There is nothing you could have told me on December 31 to make me believe that eating at a restaurant, sitting at a coffee shop, casual "retail therapy," attending sporting events, or even gathering with our family for Easter were in danger of extinction, or even temporary disruption. Essentially overnight, large events like parades and baseball games, vacations, international travel, and even attending church were banned.

By early May we were all begging for 2020 to be canceled with no refunds and no returns. But we still had over six months to go.

Memorial Day approached and we felt as if some relief was in sight. The warm weather gave hope that everything would soon return to normal. And then June rolled in like hurricane. A video surfaced of a black man with the foot of a white police officer on his neck in Minneapolis, causing protests to erupt over all the country.

These peaceful protests—guaranteed by the First Amendment of the Constitution of the United States—soon gave way to chaos, vandalism, and anarchy. Months of lockdowns exacerbated the need for people to express themselves. City after city saw unprecedented looting, burning, and destruction of businesses and personal property. Portland, Oregon; Seattle, Washington; Baltimore, MD; and Washington, DC, fared the worst.

After a week of protests and riots, something odd happened. Rather than diffusing and everyone going back to live as normal, the demonstrations intensified. Week after week protests and violence continued. Portland, Oregon, saw over 100 continual days of riots.[136] Many of the businesses burned to the ground during the unrest were owned by minorities. Clearly this was no longer about protesting the killing of an unarmed black man. The entire county seemed to be in chaos.

The unrest escalated. Calls to defund and dismantle police departments erupted across the entire country. Soon every news channel talked daily about racism and the need for "social justice" in America.

The Big Question

Is America systemically racist? That's the question. Unfortunately, many Americans are buying into this notion without even understanding what systemic racism means. My answer is yes, unfortunately there are elements of systemic racism in our county. BUT, it's not in the way you think.

The term systemic comes from the root word "system." A system of racism does not originate at retail level (with an individual). Systems are developed at the top of the pyramid with the higher positions of leadership, not the bottom.

Of course, there will always be certain individuals who act inappropriately. I don't deny individual racism exists, because it does. We all have heard about truly awful things which have been said and done to black folks and other minorities. Furthermore, I certainly don't condone it. We are all human beings created in the image of God, for whom Jesus died. But the idea that all of American society is defined by a few hateful individuals is a very different claim.

Let's look at areas of our society which are not racist first. The notion that our police institutions across the country are systematically racist is unfounded. The numbers don't support that narrative of police racism and brutality toward the black community. According to a USA Today article dated July 3, 2020, there is "no epidemic of fatal police shootings against unarmed Black Americans."[137]

The article backs its claim with the following: in 2019 only 14 unarmed black Americans were shot by police. That same year 25 white Americans were shot by police. Keep in mind that there are roughly 50 million police actions nationwide per year. Every single American—black, white, brown, or purple—has a one-in-a-million chance of being shot by the police.

Having said that, it's important to acknowledge that police officers do have a bias, but it's not against minorities. Their bias is against *criminals,* regardless of their skin color or gender. As with any profession, law enforcement tends to attract individuals with similar personality traits. A strong majority of police officers are very protective by nature. They willingly enter the field of law enforcement to serve and defend the community.

Nothing pushes the buttons of a protector quite like seeing a child who has suffered extreme neglect from a parent, or a woman being abused by her boyfriend, a teenager high on heroin needing immediate intervention to survive, or finding a dead body of a homeless man. Officers are continually forced to make complex, fast-paced, ambiguous decisions with minimal information.[138] The consistent exposure to these traumatic situations can affect an officer's mental health. Many studies have come out recently showing the connection between the continual exposure to trauma and an officer's ability to make split-second decisions.

Additionally, it's important to understand that law enforcement by nature is reactive, not proactive. Police officers don't make the laws, they just enforce them. There are no laws on the books presently which discriminate against individuals based on their ethnicity. To say that officers intentionally target minorities shows a misunderstanding of how the law works.

Yes, there are those who are racist within the ranks as with any profession or group of individuals. But the .001% of the bad apples aren't the root cause of the backlash against the police community. By now, many are beginning to recognize that the attacks on law enforcement are a smoke screen concealing the real problem, which we'll see in the next chapter.

Systemic racism also implies that minorities are denied the ability to thrive in America. This simply is not true. Ironically, professional athletes and Hollywood elites are typically the first ones to lecture on the subject of the oppression of minorities, and yet nowhere in America do we find more wealthy, successful black and brown individuals than in these two demographics!

One look at Forbes Magazine "Highest-Paid Athletes of 2020" confirms the truth that ethnicity is not a key determining factor in one's success in the field of athletics.[139] In fact, the sport these athletes compete in has more impact on their earnings than their race. Basketball players in the top 100 highest paid athletes, for example, cumulatively earned $1.2 billion, while tennis players on this list collectively made $245 million.

The notion that the average Caucasian in America is racist is also unfounded. One of the greatest evidences of this is "Just Sam," a poor, young black woman from the Frederick Douglass Houses in Harlem, New York City who used to sing in the subways to pay the bills. She won *American Idol* in 2020. This highly rated singing competition is a television series that decides its finalists based on nationwide audience voting. Just Sam was voted the number one finalist by millions of American Idol fans across the country.

Our democratic system of governance is the only one on the planet which acknowledges every human being is created equal in the sight of God and has the opportunity to pursue happiness. Our Constitution guarantees equal opportunity, but not equal outcomes.

Galatians 3:28 says, "There is no longer Jew or Gentile, slave or free, male and female. For you are all one in Christ Jesus." The Bible makes it clear that God does not play favorites. He sent his only Son to die for our sins so that ALL may have eternal life.

Divided We Stand

Remarkably, the great divide between races seems to have reappeared lately. Looking back as recently at 2016, the discussion about racial tensions seemed to be fading. Morgan Freeman, famous for his roles in *The Shawshank Redemption* and *Bruce Almighty* commented on the ridiculousness of Black History Month in an interview with Mike Wallace on CBS' *60 Minutes*.[140] During the 2008 interview, Freeman also said that the best way to end racism is to stop talking about it.

During a 2014 interview with CNN's Don Lemon, Freeman rejected the idea that being born Black in America was an obstacle. "I don't think wealth and genetics have anything to do with each other, actually," the 80-year-old Freeman said. "Put your mind to what you want to do and go from there."[141]

Even Whoopie Goldberg, host on The View, commented in 2016 that the Academy Awards "can't be that racist because she once won a prized trophy."[142] She was one of many black celebrities who denied claims of racial bias in the article.

Fast forward to 2020. Every news network is discussing racial issues, every day. An exacerbated race war has seemingly appeared out of nowhere.

Back in the Day

There was a time when American society was "systemically racist." Even though slavery was officially abolished on September 22, 1863, by President Abraham Lincoln's Emancipation Proclamation, the fight was far from over. Factions within our government continued to persecute persons of color and systematically discriminate against them for decades. These laws were intended to marginalize African

Americans by denying them the ability to hold jobs, receive an education, and vote.[143] This marks a dark time in our history.

Laws were presented and passed by individual Southern states—later known as Jim Crow Laws—beginning in the late 1870s requiring the separation of whites from "persons of color" on public transportation and in schools.[144] These principles were extended to theaters, parks, restaurants, and even cemeteries to avoid any appearance that blacks and whites were equal.

In 1896, a landmark case was tried before the United States Supreme Court. *Plessy v. Ferguson* involved the plaintiff Homer Plessy contending that his constitutional rights were being violated when he was ordered to move to the train car "for blacks." Plessy's argument was denied and segregation was upheld.[145] The *Plessy v. Ferguson* case is significant because it began the "separate-but-equal" doctrine, alleging that separate schools and transportation for blacks was legal as long as they were equal.

Finally, in 1954, the Supreme Court overturned the first legislation that kept communities segregated. In the *Brown v. Board of Education of Topeka* case the Supreme Court ruled unanimously that racial segregation of children in public schools was unconstitutional. Oliver Brown filed the suit after his daughter Linda Brown was denied entrance to Topeka's all-white elementary schools.[146]

The following year, in 1955, Rosa Parks refused to give up her seat on the bus to a white man, sparking a year-long boycott of public transportation. This boycott was led by the newly appointed pastor of Dexter Avenue Baptist church in Montgomery, Alabama—Rev. Dr. Martin Luther King, Jr. On December 20, 1956, the Supreme Court ruled on *Browder v. Gayle* and overturned racial segregation on buses, also deeming it unconstitutional.[147]

History revealed that "separate-but-equal" education, transportation, and other services were not, in fact, equal.

Since this time, the United States has made great strides toward leveling the playing field and creating opportunities for all Americans. Economic prosperity over the next few decades created an environment where nearly anyone willing to work hard and persist could succeed. Oprah Winfrey—one of the richest and most influential women in the world—for example, was born to poor, unmarried, teenaged parents. Oprah suffered repeated sexual abuse by several male relatives and friends of her mother. She eventually moved to Nashville to escape the abuse and live with her father.[148] And yet, despite the immense obstacles she faced, Oprah emerged as the first black female billionaire in America.

Many minority groups, in fact, are thriving in America. An Insider Monkey article published in March of 2018 lists the seven richest, most powerful ethnic groups in America. Russian-Americans, for example, have a median household income of $77,349. This group is superseded by Israeli-Americans at $79,736; Australian-Americans have a median household income of $81,452; Filipino-Americans with $82,389; Taiwanese-Americans at $85,566; and Jewish-Americans with a median household income of $97,500. Indian-Americans top the list with a median household income of $101,390.[149]

Policy Matters

We have a "systemic" problem in this country but it's not racism. It's poverty. We have created systems that perpetuate poverty from one generation to another.

As the Great Depression was ending, President Franklin Delano Roosevelt enacted his Social Security Act in 1935. This initiated our current welfare system by providing federal aid to the elderly, physically handicapped, and dependent mothers and children.

In 1964, Democratic President Lyndon Baines Johnson expanded this legislation by passing a series of bills as part of his "Great Society" initiative. This initiative, also known as "The War on Poverty," included a number of components:

- The Economic Opportunity Act aimed to eliminate the paradox of poverty in the midst of plenty.[150]

- The Food Stamp Act sought to use the food surplus in America to improve levels of nutrition among underserved populations.

- The Elementary and Secondary Education Act aimed to level the alleged "achievement gap" in public education.

- The Social Security Act of 1965 created Medicare and Medicaid.[151]

Although minority voters initially supported these measures, a wide gulf appeared between what under-privileged Americans hoped the legislation would achieve and what the Democratic politicians actually delivered.[152] African American communities realized the hypocrisy by the Johnson Administration and rioted the summer after the bill was passed.

The civil rights organizer Bayard Rustin said that the bill was good for ending segregation but said it did nothing to address the three major problems Negroes faced at that time: housing, jobs, and integrated schools. Because of this, Rustin commented that the frustration of these under-served communities only increased.[153]

President Ronald Reagan openly condemned the welfare system in a speech in Santa Barbara in February of 1986, denouncing it as misguided. He noted that under the current law, the federal government sets up a pregnant teen with an apartment, medical care, clothing, and food—as long as she doesn't marry or associate with the father of her child.

> We're in danger of creating a permanent culture of poverty as inescapable as any chain or bond; a second and separate America, an America of lost dreams and stunted lives... The irony is that misguided welfare programs instituted in the name of compassion have actually helped turn a shrinking problem into a national tragedy.[154]

As Reagan predicted, this legislation has attributed to an alarming phenomenon of "child mothers and absentee fathers," particularly among the poor. According to the National Vital Statistics Report published by the CDC National Center for Health Statistics, out-of-wedlock birth rates have skyrocketed since 1965. At that time, the out-of-wedlock birth rate was 25% among Blacks. This rate rose to 68% in 1991, and then escalated to 77% of black babies being born to unmarried mothers by 2015.[155]

> Our Constitution guarantees
> equal opportunity,
> but not equal outcomes.

The connection between the absence of fathers and poverty is undeniable. As noted in Chapter 7 of this book, women-only households are significantly more likely to live below the poverty line. The lack of a father in the home also greatly increases the chance a child will suffer a behavioral disorder, run away from home, be convicted of a violent offense, or end up in prison.

The "Great Society" legislation is not the only democratic policy which generated systems of poverty. Many believe that The Violent Crime and Law Enforcement Act of 1994 profoundly impacted poor communities by exacerbating the fatherlessness situation. The "Three Strikes" provision in the bill imposed mandatory life sentences for individuals with three or more felony convictions.[156] This bill sent thousands of Americans to prison for life for non-violent offenses, including offenses as minor as stealing loose change from a parked car.[157]

Even more insidious than handing out life sentences to non-violent criminals, is how the crime bill incentivized states to keep inmates jailed longer. The bill promised states $12.5 billion to build new prisons if they agreed to pass laws requiring prisoners to serve a minimum of 85% of their sentences. So, instead of focusing on rehabilitation and releasing prisoners early for good behavior, it's possible that politicians lined their own pockets by taking advantage of federal inducements.

It's understandable how this could be considered systemic racism since these policies disproportionately affect inner city minority communities. However, these policies don't affect all Black and Brown people equally, as racism implies. As discussed earlier, many minorities are thriving in America, including many who have overcome extreme poverty.

Systemic poverty is a very serious issue faced by minority communities in our country and it deserves an answer, as we'll discuss in the next chapter. Systemic *racism* in America, however, is an illusion.

During the Civil Rights Movement in the 1960s the line was clearly drawn between races, and blacks and whites were on opposite sides. The same is not true today. Many on the "social justice" side purportedly defending oppressed minorities are white, upper-middle class, young adults. Some on the opposing side saying America is not racist—but is, in fact, the land of opportunity—are themselves minorities.

I am Not Oppressed

Joel Patrick, a young, conservative black man from Ohio tells a story about an encounter with one of his customers. Patrick, who started his own landscaping business in his early 20s, was called by a homeowner to remove a tree that had fallen on his property. He was met at the door by the renter of the house, a middle-aged white woman employed as a professor at a local university.

When the woman opened the door and saw a young black man standing there, Patrick relays how the woman gasped and said how sorry she felt for him. He was very confused by her reaction but didn't respond. The woman continued with how terrible it must be for him, as a black man, *to be oppressed in America.* She said she teaches her students everyday about systemic racism and oppression, and she couldn't imagine what he was going through.

Still confused, Patrick shrugged off her remarks and continued with the appraisal, since that was his purpose for being called to the house. Later, while reflecting on the encounter, he commented to his one million viewers on Instagram how *he is not oppressed.* The woman apparently didn't understand that this so-called oppressed black man was an entrepreneur, and had driven to this call in his late model Ram 1500 TRX 4x4 Crew Cab with special-order orange metallic paint truck which probably cost more than the house she was renting.[158]

Patrick posted this quote weeks later: "Some people take a single brick, learn to lay it, and build a business...while others take a single brick, throw it through a glass window, and complain about inequality."[159]

Why, then, does the media continue to talk about the race war in America? They belabor the conversation on how the majority is oppressing the minority, instead of holding accountable the politicians who enacted these oppressive policies which served themselves, rather than the communities entrusted to them.

In recent years it's becoming clear that the divide is between those who *think* differently, not between those who *look* differently. The real story is how individuals holding opposite political views can reach radically different conclusions when presented with the same set of facts. Unfortunately, social media and media networks are complicit with creating this divide.

Racism isn't a universal truth, it's a political construct. It's man-made. According to Dinesh D'Souza, award-winning filmmaker and best-selling author,

> Racism is the witchcraft of the 21st century. Now, as then, it's hard to find witches. Many people haven't actually seen a witch. Yet powerful people create public hysteria and insist witches are everywhere. Some are invisible! Now, as then, it's about power and social control.[160]

The Wrap Up

It's not our police force, laws, or other people that are preventing individuals from achieving the American dream. Rather, it is ideologies such as victimhood, entitlement, group think, and others that keep many stuck in an imaginary prison of ideas, rather than a true victim of a corrupt and intolerant system. Many of these ideologies are being pushed by political leaders and the media.

Orlando Patterson, a Jamaican-born American sociologist and professor at Harvard University said,

> America is now the least racist white major-ity society in the world; it has a better record of legal protection of minorities than any other society, white or black; [and] offers more opportunities to a greater number of black persons than any other society, including all of Africa.[161]

America is not systemically racist, but there are a few individuals from every ethnic group who spew hatred and intolerance. This tiny minority does not represent the majority of Americans, but they are receiving the largest amount of airtime on TV and social media.

In the words of Morgan Freeman, "The best way to end racism is to stop talking about it."

Poverty, however, is a systemic issue and policy matters! Legislation has a powerful impact on cre-ating systems of both wealth and poverty. We have to demand better from our lawmakers. We'll explore in the next chapter, "Social Injustice," how the Trump Administration is actively rolling back many oppressive policies which have plagued our minority communities.

We'll also discuss in Chapter 13 how no one cares for the poor, oppressed, and marginalized more that God, and how our responsibility as believers in Jesus Christ is to do the same.

America is far from perfect, but we've made great strides to correct injustices which are contrary to our constitutional guarantees. The "American dream" is still open for business and on the menu for anyone with the will to work for it, regardless of the color of your skin.

DISCUSSION GUIDE

Chapter 12: Race is On

The purpose of this section is to help you facilitate a meaningful discussion surrounding the material in this chapter. Please refer to Appendix: Tips for Leading Small Group Discussions.

1. Can you summarize the main idea of this chapter?

2. Do you believe that America is systemically racist? Explain your position.

3. Why do you think that some ethnic groups in America are thriving more than others?

4. Consider this: "In recent years it's becoming clear that the divide is between those who *think* differently, not between those who *look* differently." Do you agree or disagree?

5. Do you agree or disagree that race is a political construct? Defend your position.

6. "America is now the least racist white majority society in the world; it has a better record of legal protection of minorities than any other society; [and] offers more opportunities to a greater number of black persons than any other society, including all of Africa." Why do you believe this is so?

Scriptures to read and discuss:

- Galatians 3:28
- Romans 2:11
- James 2:9
- Acts 10:34–35
- John 3:16

Social Injustice

The tragic death of George Floyd sent shock waves throughout the country. The call for "action for racial justice—to empower, support, and accelerate immediate solutions, as well as work toward long-term systematic transformation"[162] resonated throughout the United States.

But as time progressed, it became apparent that many of those protesting weren't looking for immediate solutions or long-term systematic transformation—they were looking for anarchy. As cities burned, one prominent political group took center stage by exploiting the chaos—Black Lives Matter (BLM).

The seemingly organic demonstrations soon gave way to "mostly peaceful protests" and/or full-on riots in many major cities in America. Arsonists set fire to retail stores, police departments, vehicles, restaurants, and even federal buildings in Portland,

Seattle, New York City, Chicago, and many other cities nationwide. Pictures of decimated businesses flooded the internet. Damages from looting and vandalism totaled more than $2 billion.[163]

Overnight, these demonstrations evolved into calls to "defund the police." Within weeks, the BLM organization secured pledges from Corporate America in the amount of $1.678 billion.[164] Bank of America, for example, pledged $1 million. Nike, Sony Music Group, and Walmart pledged $100 thousand. Google, Amazon, Spotify, and Facebook—not surprisingly—also wanted a part of the action and pledged thousands of dollars.

What is Social Justice

Many individuals and organizations sincerely wanted to help those oppressed by our "systemically racist culture" in America. As a result, many people, corporations, organizations, and even churches have jumped on the social justice bandwagon.

Given recent events, many of us are contemplating what exactly is social justice and what does it accomplish? Why does it suddenly appear that after decades of prosperity for Americans from all ethnic and socioeconomic backgrounds, many now can't seem to find justice?

Consider the following definition of social justice:

> Social justice is a political and philosophical theory which asserts that there are dimensions to the concept of justice beyond those embodied in the principles of civil or criminal law,

economic supply and demand, or traditional moral frameworks. Social justice tends to focus more on just relations between groups within society as opposed to the justice of individual conduct or justice for individuals.

Historically and in theory, the idea of social justice is that all people should have equal access to wealth, health, well-being, justice, privileges, and opportunity regardless of their legal, political, economic, or other circumstances. In modern practice, social justice revolves around favoring or punishing different groups of the population, regardless of any given individual's choices or actions, based on value judgements regarding historical events, current conditions, and group relations. In economic terms, this often means redistribution of wealth, income, and economic opportunities from groups whom social justice advocates consider to be oppressors to those whom they consider to be the oppressed. Social justice is often associated with identity politics, socialism, and revolutionary communism.[165]

One reason social justice is so troubling is because it's not interested in solving problems and creating solutions. Rather, it's about arbitrarily "favoring and punishing different groups of the population, regardless of any given individual's choices or actions" (see definition above). It's the opposite of true justice; it subverts the natural order and, as a result, favors the strong while exploiting the weak. It's anti-justice in essence.

Consider the call to defund the police. Many believe this began with Floyd's death, but it didn't. Would you be surprised to learn that this movement began in the early 1900s?[166] Dr. Michael Sawyer, and associate professor at Colorado College explains that the "abolition-democracy" is all about abolishing the institutions which oppress African Americans, and has been around for over a century. The issue of "systemic police violence" and the need to eliminate funding for these institutions first appeared in articles from the editor of Crisis Magazine in 1910. [167]

This movement gained national attention in 2015 when then President Obama advocated for disbanding traditional police agencies and focusing on community policing.[168]

The reality, however, is that the notion of disbanding police departments is not supported by the minority communities who have the most to lose. According to Newsweek, 81% of Black Americans don't want less police in their neighborhoods. As much as 20% of minorities want more of a police presence in their communities.[169]

The city of Memphis, Tennessee, for example, had a crime rate in 2019 of 84-per-one- thousand residents, making it one of the ten most dangerous cities in America. Individuals have a 1-in-12 chance of being a victim of violent crime, including murder, rape, robbery, and assault. A Memphis resident also has a 1-in-15 chance of being a victim of property crime, including burglary, theft, and motor vehicle theft.[170]

Following the unrest in the summer of 2020, several major cities witnessed a sharp spike in murders, according to Forbes Magazine.[171] While some have claimed no connection between reducing funding and manpower for police departments and increases in crime, there appears to be plenty of correlation. Several of the cities that began cutting funding for police departments—Chicago, New York, Philadelphia, Atlanta, and Washington D.C.—saw alarming increases in homicides.[172]

New York City, for instance, made the news when Mayor Bill de Blasio slashed $1 billion from the NYPD budget in June of 2020, and canceled a 1,200-person police recruiting class set to start the following month. The city saw a 77% increase in murder in the first six months of 2020, compared to all of 2019.[173]

Justice in Action

True justice is an action, not a philosophical ideology. As discussed in the previous chapter, decades of poor legislation oppressed many Black and Latino communities. The Three-Strikes provision in the 1994 Crime Bill increased sentences for non-violent drug offenders and made it more difficult for prisoners to be granted parole.

The Crime Bill imposed tougher sentences for those caught with crack-cocaine than those caught with powder cocaine. This disparity also seems to target minorities. According to former Rep. Keith Ellison, "Whites use cocaine, blacks use crack."[174] Whites, according to this equation, get probation, blacks get a decade behind bars.[175]

One individual caught up by the stricter sentencing guidelines resulting from the Crime Bill was Alice Marie Johnson. She was convicted in 1996 for her involvement with a crack- cocaine trafficking organization in Memphis, Tennessee. She was subsequently sentenced to life in prison without parole, even though this was her first offense. Johnson admitted her involvement with the drug trafficking organization but said that she didn't actually sell drugs or make drug deals. [176]

Johnson's case was brought to the attention of President Trump in 2018. Two weeks later—after serving 22 years in a federal prison—Johnson was granted clemency by the President and released from prison in June of that year. Johnson was a model prisoner during her time and became an ordained minister while incarcerated.

In order to systematically address the injustices imposed by the 1994 Crime Bill, President Trump signed into law The First Step Act (P.L. 115-391) in December of 2018. The legislation drew widespread, bi-partisan support. This law seeks to improve criminal justice outcomes by creating new mechanisms for maintaining public safety and decreasing the size of the federal prison population. [177] This new law creates incentives for good behavior and participating in rehabilitation programs. Under this new directive, federal inmates convicted of non-violent crimes can earn up to 54 days of credit for every year of their *imposed* sentence, rather than every year of their served sentence. [178] This provision expedites the release of those who demonstrate model behavior, particularly those with extreme sentences.

The First Step Act of 2018 also includes humane measures. For example, the Federal Bureau of Prisons is required to house inmates as close to their primary residence as possible and practical. Some terminally ill and elderly prisoners can be granted home confinement for the remainder of their sentences.[179]

Leo Terrell, a civil rights attorney and lifelong Democrat, commended President Trump and his Administration for doing more for the black community during his first four years in office than all previous administrations combined in the last 50 years.[180]

The Author of Justice

No one cares more for the poor, oppressed, and marginalized than God, the Creator of the universe and Author of mankind. God created social justice—it's called the natural order. God established justice for our protection.

"Learn to do good; seek justice, correct oppression; bring justice to the fatherless, plead the widow's case" (Isaiah 1:17 ESV).

Scripture is clear about the way to achieve justice: do good, avoid evil, and help the oppressed. Justice in the Bible is not a vaguely defined concept; it's a measurement, and The Ten Commandments are the measuring stick. Psalms and Proverbs include many references to "just scales" and "true judgements."

It baffles me how people within our culture—including pastors and spiritual leaders—think that in order to achieve social justice our country needs to fundamentally change. Many church leaders encouraged their congregations to march with Black Lives Matter to protest racial inequality, rather than take solid actions to correct injustice.

There is no greater guide to social justice than the Constitution of the United States, and no other government on the planet that protects human rights more than America. The United States is the only country to offer "equal protection under the law." The idea that you could defend yourself against injustice doesn't even exist in many parts of the world. If you doubt this, I encourage you to speak to those who have fled from Cuba, the Soviet Union, or Iran to come to America.

> "Learn to do good; seek justice, correct oppression; bring justice to the fatherless, plead the widow's case."
> - Isaiah 1:17 ESV

Could it be that many of our leaders calling for "fundamental change in America" aren't looking for justice, but instead looking for control? Social justice is an intentionally vague concept that can neither be proven nor disproven. It doesn't provide a measuring stick, but instead creates an excuse for violence and vandalism when someone doesn't get their way.

State of the Church

Many churches in America are in a peculiar position right now. By siding with the social justice movement, many have unknowingly engaged in political activism without understanding the implications. At the same time, many of these churches refuse to call out the evils in our society from the pulpit, such as partial-birth abortion and the demonic nature of sex trafficking and pedophilia, for example. Many ministers declined to encourage their congregants to vote—the very foundation of our democratic society—for fear of alienating "the other side." Their silence is deafening.

During the leadup to the presidential election of 2020, Pastor Jeremiah Johnson made a bold declaration:

> The Republican National Convention is exposing the cowardice and passivity of the American Church. Is the republican party more awake than the American church? How is the RNC willing to confront issues such as abortion, racism, and bring a clear gospel message, but the church won't? This isn't about being Republican or Democrat, it's about WHO is willing to boldly address issues from a biblical standard.[181]

To be fair, the modern church movement toward utilizing a corporation-model for establishing megachurches and multi-site churches has done a lot to spread the gospel of Jesus Christ and draw in formerly disenfranchised individuals. The church in

America continues to do a spectacular job of caring for the oppressed. As mentioned in the "Capital Gains" chapter, Christians feed the poor, provide housing for the homeless, and offer services to the underserved all around the world.

But the downside to the expansion of the church in America is the normalization of a Christian subculture that is divorced in many ways from the traditional values the Bible embraces. Christianity used to be inexplicably tied to conservatism; the belief that marriage is between one man and one woman, abortion is murder, there are only two genders, the sexual exploitation of minors (e.g., pedophilia) is to be condemned, and that God is King, not the government. But this is no longer true. Anyone making these claims from the pulpit would be branded as a "hater" or "anti-LGBTQ" and their church would be boycotted or canceled. Pastors are concerned with disenfranchising their members.

Furthermore, the government has set restrictions on our churches, and admittedly, we've allowed it. The 501(c)(3) status sought by churches because of the tax-exempt benefit ties these organizations to more government regulations. This is the exact fear our Founding Fathers addressed in the First Amendment to the Constitution.

Some pastors, however, have spoken out against the government overreach through oppressive lockdowns in the midst of the panic of the global pandemic. Two California pastors—Jack Hibbs of Calvary Chapel in Chino Hills and Rob McCoy of Calvary Chapel in Thousand Oaks—from the Non-Essential Movement (founded by Kirk Cameron and Ryan Higgins) have stood up to protest the infringement of our religious freedoms and to sound a warning against Marxist and socialist ideology creeping into our government.

Other local pastors are taking risks, as well, to stand up for conservative values such as Greg Locke from Global Vision Bible Church and Ron Bailey from New Beginnings Church. Many pastors, however, are choosing to remain silent.

The American church is charging full speed ahead toward the cliff of irrelevance when it refuses to call out blatant immorality in our culture. Local pastors aren't expected to directly impact Hollywood, Wall-Street, or even Washington, DC. They are expected, however, to direct and persuade those sitting in their pews and auditoriums each week. If our religious leaders aren't sounding the alarm to those within their own sphere of influence, our moral compass will forever be tainted.

Policy, more than any other vehicle, profoundly impacts our culture. Consider the enormous influence that the 1962 ruling to end school prayer, the 2014 ruling that the Ten Commandments couldn't be displayed in court buildings, and the 2015 ruling that all same-sex unions must be recognized nationwide had—and still have—on current culture.

The reluctance of the church to engage in the policy discussions further solidifies the Christian subculture. This situation has created several generations of Christians who do not hold—and may not even understand—a biblical worldview. A Barna Group study concluded that only 9% of individuals who identified as born-again Christians identify as having a biblical worldview.[182] *Only 9%.* Your world-view has a profound impact on how you view moral issues and how you perceive truth.

This means that people sitting in church pews and auditoriums week after week are not being instructed on how the Ten Commandments, the teachings of the Prophets, and the Apostle Paul's writings and instructions to new believers should direct how we protect human life, value religious freedom, properly view sexuality, and project these values in our current culture.

Instead, we hear lessons filled with popular psychology on a weekly basis informing us how to become better people and get along with our neighbors. There is nothing wrong with this, of course, but it's only half of the message. God loves justice as much as He does mercy; He promises judgement as much as He promises provision. We're directed to be *both* "innocent as doves" and "shrewd as serpents." [183]

By abdicating our responsibility as Christian leaders to educate those within our circles of influence, the modern American church is culpable of permitting our culture to revert back to the time of the Judges in the Old Testament where "everyone does what is right in his own eyes."[184]

The good news is that revival is coming to America. The bad news is that it may not be coming through the church.

Rogan O'Handley, a former Corporate Finance Attorney and civil rights activist from St. Petersburg, FL said on Instagram, "God is making a comeback in America."[185]

Kayleigh McEnany, the White House Press Secretary under the Trump Administration is very bold about her relationship with Jesus Christ and told CBN news that she believes that God put her in the White House for a reason.[186]

Abby Johnson, former Planned Parenthood Director turned Pro-Life, "I wish people were more concerned about offending the heart of God as they are about offending each other."[187]

Kevin McGary, an Information Technology professional with 35 years of experience in Cybersecurity, Enterprise Applications, and Application Development Automation said this at the Well Versed Conference in September 2020, "We don't need a racial reconciliation; we need a biblical and spiritual reconciliation."

Bevelyn Beatty, a young black woman in New York City with a troubled past, together with her friend Edmee, poured gallons and gallons of black paint to cover the Black Lives Matter "mural" in downtown Manhattan. Bevelyn and Edmee yelled "only Jesus Matters" while protesting BLM and the Mayor of New York City's disrespect and degradation of their police department.

Even President Trump himself, in one of his campaign rallies in October of 2020, named Jesus Christ and referred to him as "the Boss."

I never thought I would see the day when political activists—not pastors and church leaders—would boldly declare the name of Jesus and the truth of the gospel from the podium. I could never picture how social media (even with all of its ills) and political rallies would be more effective platforms for sharing the Good News than the pulpit. I wouldn't have imagined that a United States President would be a greater champion for the unborn child than the Evangelical Church. President Trump has done more for the Christian community than the Christian church has done for itself.

The Church needs to wake up, or she will be left behind.

The Wrap-Up

The only way to achieve true social justice is to move back *toward* our Constitution—the document founded on the ideals of human rights as presented in Scripture. It is essential that we move *toward* the principles that create law and order, rather than moving further away from it.

Defunding police departments has tragic effects for inner city populations, as history has shown. Many urban communities want more police protection, not less. It would appear that the majority of Americans—particularly the most vulnerable—favor true justice over the vague "philosophical theory" of social justice rooted in revolutionary Communism.

America is headed down a very dark path if we continue to seek "fundamental change" to the rule of law. There is no peace without safety, and there is no safety without justice.

The Lord loves justice. "Turn away from evil and do good, and you will live in the land forever. For the Lord loves justice; he will never abandon the godly. He will keep them safe forever, but the children of the wicked will die. The godly will possess the land and will live there forever" (Psalm 37:27–29).

DISCUSSION GUIDE

Chapter 13: Social Injustice

The purpose of this section is to help you facilitate a meaningful discussion surrounding the material in this chapter. Please refer to Appendix: Tips for Leading Small Group Discussions.

1. Can you summarize the main idea of this chapter?

2. In your own words, give the definition of social justice.

3. How is social justice the same as or different from justice as defined in Scripture?

4. Do you personally hold a biblical worldview? How does a biblical worldview affect one's attitudes and actions?

5. What does the phrase "equal protection under the law" mean? In which countries does this exist?

6. What are your thoughts about the "defund the police" movement? Would you support it for your city?

Scriptures to read and discuss:

- Isaiah 1:17
- Zechariah 7:9
- Proverbs 28:5
- Proverbs 106:3
- Deuteronomy 16:20
- Psalm 58:11

What in the World

With Tammy Summers

I view December 2019 much the same as I look back on August 2001, or how I would have thought about November 1941 had I been alive during the attack on Pearl Harbor. These dates mark a time in American history before the world changed forever, and there was no returning to things as we knew it.

When I was a teenager, I remember reading the book of Revelation in the Bible the same way I read George Orwell's *1984*—as science fiction. I couldn't picture any global event—war, natural catastrophe, or even a nuclear bomb—who's impact could affect the entire world at the same time. This would never happen in my lifetime, I concluded.

And then the Coronavirus pandemic originating in China spread to 180 countries worldwide, according to the World Health Organization.[188]

The one-world government needed to usher in the Anti-Christ also seemed far-fetched. As an American, I had a nearly impossible time picturing a scenario where one body would rule over all the countries. I could see this happening in Eastern Europe or Africa, as in the case of British Colonialism, but could never envision every country being under one ruler.

And then a video appeared on social media in 2020 of American politicians from both parties over the past twenty years talking about the need for a "New World Order."[189] China, one member said, needs to be brought into the New World Order; Ted Turner stated that the United Nations should be the global police.

Nowadays, future events predicted by the Bible to occur in the last days sound peculiarly similar to the evening news. Even though there has always been political tension, environmental disasters, and racial division in our country, this is different. Recent events have unleashed chaos in unprecedented ways.

The intent of this chapter isn't to debate theological positions related to biblical prophecy, or to say that Jesus is coming back tomorrow. However, the apparent connection between current events and future events predicted in Scripture is too similar to regard as coincidence. I don't believe in coincidence. I believe that God is trying to capture our attention.

Bible prophecy predicts exactly what is unfolding before our eyes. Jesus tells us to be alert and watch for the signs of his coming. If God didn't want us to know the circumstances surrounding the return of

Jesus, He wouldn't have told us. But He did. There are numerous signs coming to pass in society, nature, technology, politics, and spiritually that are pointing to the Lord's return.

Since 2014, God has displayed some of the most spectacular heavenly events that we have witnessed in our lifetimes. In Matthew 24, Jesus prophesies that in the end times there will be signs in the heavens that will point to his soon return and lead to the repentance of many.

The blood moon tetrads of 2014 and 2015 fell on the Jewish Feast of Trumpet and Atonement. A total solar eclipse was observed for some of the world on August 21, 2017. Ironically, this solar eclipse coincided with five of the worst hurricanes in recorded history which affected hundreds of thousands of people and caused billions of dollars in damage. Hurricane Harvey, a Category 4 storm hit Texas in late August and caused $125 billion in damages expanding into Kentucky, Mississippi, Louisiana, and Tennessee. Hurricane Irma, a Category 5 storm, was the largest Atlantic storm in recorded history and caused catastrophe damage in Antigua, Bahamas, US Virgin Islands, and Barbuda. Hurricane Jose, a Category 4 hurricane, affected Bermuda, Nova Scotia, and the east coast of the United States causing $2.84 million in damages. Hurricane Maria, a Category 5 storm, hit the Dominican Republic causing over 400 deaths. Furthermore, Hurricane Fernanda, a Category 4 storm, recorded the strongest wind gusts on the East Pacific.[190]

The Bible indicates that the sun, moon, and stars do far more than mark physical time; they can reveal what is scheduled on God's agenda and his appointed times.

Just as the Scriptures predict, we are seeing an increase of earthquakes in diverse places with greater intensity and frequency. Droughts, fires, and flooding of enormous magnitude are devastating the world. The Smithsonian Institute reported in September of 2020 that there have been more shakings under the earth and volcanic eruptions in the past five years than in the past 300 years.[191]

Pestilences such as COVID-19, Ebola, and the H1N1 virus (Swine Flu) have taken the lives of millions globally. Revelation 6:8 predicts that a fourth of the earth will die in the last days, primarily from hunger. In the poorest areas of the world, such as Sub-Saharan Africa and parts of the Middle East, COVID-19 is referred to as the "hunger virus" because many more are dying of starvation than from the illness associated with Coronavirus.

The Bible predicts that many will suffer despair in the last days. 2 Timothy 3 reveals how people will be in love with self, pleasure, and money like as in the days of Noah in the Bible where they were drinking, partying, and living in sexual perversion and immorality; then sudden destruction came. We are seeing suicide rates accelerating rapidly. Tragically, an average of 191 people died every day of 2018 in the United States from the opioid crisis.[192]

The globe isn't experiencing a few prophetic indicators, but a convergence of many signs on the prophetic list.

Those who speak out about the prophetic warning signs that we are watching receive the typical backlash from anti-religious groups, the media, and sadly even those among the church. Jesus warned that in the last days, haters would say, "Where is the promise of his coming?" Many will mock them saying there have always been wars, pestilences, and earthquakes.

> The globe isn't experiencing a few prophetic indicators, but a convergence of many signs on the prophetic list.

God gives us prophecies of the coming events *to prepare, not scare.* Looking back to the biblical times, God never poured out his wrath before his warning. God gave Noah 120 years advance notice to build the ark before the great flood. Noah and his family entered the ark and closed the door before the wrath of God was poured out upon the earth.

God sent Jonah to warn the pagan city of Nineveh. When their initial repentance didn't take and they returned to their evil ways, God sent Nahum 150 years later to the Assyrian city to warn them again before sending judgement. Because of God's character and great love for us, He is warning us now while we still have the opportunity to repent.

The One to Watch

The most significant current events correlating with End Time prophecies are happening with Israel. In the 1980s the automobile maker Renault, headquartered in France, displayed their slogan, "The one to watch" in the rear window of all of their cars. If the world's stage was a vast expanse of car companies, then Israel would be the Renault Auto Groupe—the one to watch.

The nation of Israel, located in Western Asia on the northern shore of the Red Sea and the southeastern shore of the Mediterranean Sea, borders Lebanon, Syria, Jordan, and the Palestinian territories. Its population is estimated to be close to 8 million people, and the size of Israel can be compared to the state of New Jersey.[193] This relatively tiny country is central to understanding prophecy regarding the End Times.

Israel is centrally located in the Middle East—the region of the world which has been in conflict for the last two millennium. Religious wars between Sunnis and Shiite Muslims have been brewing for ages. Saudi Arabia and Iran are engaged in fighting for control over the region.

Ever since declaring its independence as a nation in 1948, the rest of the Muslim world has treated Israel with hostility. Despite the immense hatred for the Jewish people by those who hold to Islam, much of Europe, and even the United States, Israel continues to rise as the superpower of the Middle East.

The Spoils

Why are the Jews so hated by the world? Why are the Arabs surrounding Israel threatening and fighting against their neighbor? What does Israel have that they don't? The answer is found in Ezekiel 38. The prophecy contained in this chapter indicates that Israel's enemies are after "the spoil," not the land, nor to challenge the nation's religion. The "spoil" equals oil and natural gas. In 2010, Israel discovered over 16 trillion cubic feet of natural gas, estimated to be worth over $95 billion.[194]

Israel has solicited countries to invest in their gas fields, building relationships with India, Greece, and Cyprus. These nations are collaborating with Israel on the new gas pipeline that runs from the Mediterranean Sea, through Cyprus, Greece, and Italy to Western Europe.

The list of Israel's allies continues to grow. Prime Minister of Israel, Benjamin Netanyahu, has recently aligned with Visegrad Group (V4) consisting of the nations of Hungary, Czech Republic, Poland, and Slovakia on the issue of energy innovation.[195] Netanyahu also visited Uganda, Rwanda, Kenya, and Ethiopia in July 2016 to discuss business opportunities. The relationship between Israel and African countries was strong in the 1960s but was strained by the 1973 Arab-Israeli war, and further severed when Israel partnered with the apartheid regime in South Africa before its fall in 1994.[196]

Israel's new partnerships around its natural gas pipeline is infuriating the Russians. Russia were secretly implementing their own pipeline project, Nord Stream 2. This pipeline was 93% complete when it came to a total halt after Angela Merkel of Germany pulled out their financial support. Merkel decided to withdraw support from Russia after President Trump exposed her plan and threatened sanctions on Germany.[197]

The United States, who previously provided 22% of NATO's funding, is applying pressure to Germany—the strongest economy among European NATO nations—because of their failure to contribute 2% of its GDP to the collective NATO budget. The United States is concerned that partnering with Vladimir Putin and Russia on its Nord Stream 2 pipeline would compromise Germany by increasing Putin's influence over Merkel. Many feel that Merkel is personally receiving kickbacks from the pipeline deal.

Much of Europe is also concerned about Germany's partnership with Russia. Denmark, for example, stopped the drilling under their territory by rejecting construction project permits in its territorial waters.[198] European leaders feared that an aggressive Moscow would not hesitate to use the gas supply as a diplomatic weapon. Partnering with the United Sates and Israel pipeline presents a safer and more lucrative business arrangement for European nations.

The Trump Card

Israel's return to a place of prominence in the Middle East occurred when the Trump Presidency began in 2016, marking a renewed relationship with our top ally in this region. As a devoted ally to Israel, the United States moved the US embassy to Jerusalem on May 14, 2018, on the 70th anniversary of the rebirth of their nation. President Trump declared Jerusalem to be the eternal capital of Israel.

Prime Minister Netanyahu said to President Trump, "You have the key to the hearts of the people of Israel because of all the great things you have done for the Jewish State and the Jewish people." Because of President Trump's love and support for Israel, the religious Sanhedrin minted silver coins with King Cyrus and Donald Trump. (Cyrus was the king of Persia [modern day Iran] who liberated the Jewish people from their captivity in Babylon in 540 B.C.)[199]

America is reaping the blessings from this new relationship. The word of God is very clear that those who bless Israel will be blessed and those who curse Israel will be cursed (Numbers 24:9). Israel is the apple of God's eye. Those who attack Israel will suffer divine judgement.

Additionally, the Trump Administration pulled out of the 2015 Iran Nuclear deal entered into by the Obama Administration, calling it disastrous. The Iran deal threatened the stability of Israel by pushing Iran closer to the development of a nuclear weapon. While some contest this assertion, the British Broadcasting Corporation (BBC News) reported that Iran's GDP grew 12.5% and Iran's falling currency stabilized the year after the deal was implemented,[200] providing a boost to the Iranian Nuclear Program. Although Iran prospered during the Obama- era, the United States has applied harsh sanctions on Iran since 2016 in order to pressure Tehran into changing its aggressive behavior towards Israel.

The United States also withdrew from the UN Human Rights Council after Iran was praised by many UN member countries for contending that Iranian citizens are "equally protected by the law." In contrast, Amnesty International claims that Iran is guilty of crimes against humanity and is a serial abuser of human rights. US Ambassador Nikki Haley classified this move by the UN as part of its "chronic anti-Israel bias."[201]

Psalm 83 shows us how Israel's enemies will attack in an attempt to wipe them off the map, preventing them from being a nation. Their plan is for the name of Israel "to be remembered no more." The words of the psalmist are being played out at the end of these last days. Iranian leadership has been threatening Israel for years, calling them a cancerous tumor, swine, racists, and a colonial regime that promotes terrorism.

The major shift in the Middle East in recent times is described by many as a "warm peace" deal. The United States, acting as mediator between the United Arab Emirates–Israel and Bahrain–Israel, brokered a peace treaty called the Abraham Accords at the White House on September 15, 2020. In October that year, a partnership between Sudan and Israel was secured.[202] More Arab states could soon be added to the list of those who recognize and formally normalize relations with Israel.

This peace agreement between Israel, the United Arab Emirates, and Bahrain is significant to the End Times picture because President Trump did not allow one piece of the land of Israel to be divided as part of this new deal. He and his advisers understand that Joel 3:2 promises judgement for those who divide Israel.

The Palestinians, however, did not agree to this peace deal which would normalize economic and diplomatic relations between the two entities.

Power Play

The energy wars and middle eastern alliances are playing right into Bible prophecy. Israel is now prosperous, strong, and feeling safe and secure which is required for the onset of the war prophesied in Ezekiel 38, as we'll discuss in a minute. Before this war can take place, Israel needs to be at the "center" or heart of the world, a condition which did not exist until recently.[203]

As Israel continues its ascent, the remainder of the Middle East is imploding. Unprecedented turmoil began in 2011 when then-President Obama backed protesters in Tahrir Square in Cairo, Egypt and encouraged them to overthrow President Hosni Mubarak. Rather than continuing to work with Mubarak to facilitate a peaceful transition of power, Obama went on television the night of February 1, 2011, and said the transition "must begin now."[204] The Muslim Brotherhood—the strongest opposition force in Egypt—moved in to take advantage of the chaos.

The movement, instead of establishing peace and correcting the human rights abuses as many had hoped, sent the country spiraling out of control. Thousands were massacred in the months that followed, including 2,000 killed months later when Egyptian military forces fired on protesters.[205]

This uprising in Egypt is only a part of a mass-political movement known as the Arab Spring. The new awareness that revolutionary forces could topple even seemingly stable regimes swept through Yemen, Syria, Libya, and Tunisia. Ruthless dictators "[clung] to their privilege at any cost, including brutal police and military repression, and massacres of their own populations."[206] The World Bulletin publication estimates that as many as 180,000 were killed in these revolts, and 6 million displaced.[207] This movement destabilized the region for decades to come.

Boiling Point

In the last days, the Bible says that Israel will become "a cup of trembling." Their enemies will surround them on all sides. As Israel continues to build a coalition with the United States and parts of Europe over their gas and oil explorations, neighboring countries are aligning against her.

In July of 2020, President Erdogan of Turkey made a radical statement that he is planning to "take back the holy places of Jerusalem" and essentially put an end to Christendom and Israel.[208] Erdogan is also making claims that everything conquered by the Ottoman Empire over a century ago rightfully belongs to Turkey. The list of territories includes Austria, Hungary, Greece, parts of Ukraine, Iraq, Syria, Israel, and parts of North Africa, including Libya and Egypt.[209]

This seemingly random act of aggression toward the Jewish nation was sparked when Israel discovered the natural gas surplus. Turkey began desperately searching for their own gas and oil supply in the territorial waters of Greece, asserting that they rightfully own this land. However, the rest of the world disagrees with this unlawful claim and views this unauthorized exploration by the Turkish government as an act of aggression. Because Greece's military cannot stand against Turkey, this will force the other countries to take sides. Since both Greece and Turkey are part of NATO, there are no natural alliances.[210] Because of this conflict and more, many geo-political experts predict that the Middle East will explode in the coming years, at the same time that Israel is progressing with peace.

It's evident by the alignment of the middle eastern nations against Israel, that this tipping point is about to spill over into the battle mentioned prophetically in

Ezekiel 38. Although experts don't agree on precisely which nations are references in the text, many reputable scholars would agree that Iran, Turkey, and Russia are part of the collusion which attack Israel.

The Wrap-Up

We are living in a time of chaos and uncertainty. Fear has gripped the hearts and minds of millions throughout the world. Good is considered evil and evil is considered good. Lawlessness fills the streets, as the police force is slowly losing their position of authority and cities burn to the ground. Hatred for "the truth" floods every social media site. People are in love with themselves, pleasure, and money like in the days of Noah when they were drinking, partying, and living in sexual perversion and immorality, then sudden destruction came.

The nation of Israel—as predicted—is coming center-stage in the political arena. Meanwhile, the Middle East is quickly crumbling. The Bible tells us that they talk about peace but make war, with respect to the middle eastern nations.

The United States is on the right side of history when it aligns with Israel. Psalm 122:6 says, "Pray for the peace of Jerusalem: May those who love you be secure" (NIV).

The world's political arena has provided us with many signs leading to the soon return of Jesus. He warned us saying, "Nation would rise against nation and kingdom against kingdom. There will be earthquakes in various places, and famines. These are the beginning of birth pains" (Mark 13:8 NIV). These birth pains, or "sorrows" as another translation describes, are leading to a moment when all will be made right and the pain of this life will be forgotten.

Are we saying that Jesus is coming back this month, this year, or even this decade? No, we are not. We are simply asserting that the "birth pains" or times of sorrow are increasing, and Jesus' return is closer than ever before. While He walked the earth, Jesus called out the religious leaders because they could interpret the appearance of the sky but couldn't read the signs of the times.[211] If we can predict the weather, we should be able to interpret the signals God is sending us through nature to indicate Jesus is coming back soon.

In these crazy days we're living in, many are wondering—what in the world?

DISCUSSION GUIDE

Chapter 14: What in the World

The purpose of this section is to help you facilitate a meaningful discussion surrounding the material in this chapter. Please refer to Appendix: Tips for Leading Small Group Discussions.

1. Can you summarize the main idea of this chapter?

2. "God gives us prophecies of the coming events *to prepare, not scare.*" Does the discussion of end-time prophecy scare you? Why or not?

3. Do you see any other fulfillments of prophecies happening today? Can you name some events which happen in the "last days"?

4. How have the gas and oil wars affected the Middle East?

5. Discuss any recent events in the news surrounding the nation of Israel.

6. Is there anything you personally need to do to prepare for the second return of Jesus?

Scriptures to read and discuss:

• Ezekiel 38 (entire chapter)

• Mark 13 (entire chapter)

End-Time prophecy is a very complex subject. The purpose of this chapter is to encourage you to become educated about current events, particularly those happening in the Middle East which directly relate to biblical prophecy.

Conclusion

There is so much "noise" all around us. Loud voices are telling us what to think, who to believe, and how to feel. In recent years we've seen how the media attempts to control the narrative and suppress the facts. CEOs of the most prominent social media platforms confess to manipulating truth in order to control the thoughts and behaviors of their followers.

As believers in Jesus Christ, it is increasingly more difficult to know and understand the truth. Matthew 24:24 says, "For false messiahs and false prophets will rise up and perform great signs and wonders as to deceive, if possible, even God's chosen ones."

Our current situation reminds me of the climactic scene in the Wizard of Oz when Dorothy and her cohorts arrive at the Emerald City. The Great Wizard promised to grant their wishes if they could defeat the wicked witch. As they stand before the "Great and

Powerful Oz" lights flash, fire explodes, and his voice booms. The anticipation builds as they know all of their hopes will finally be realized.

And then *it* happens. Dorothy's Yorkshire Terrier, Toto, wonders away and pulls back the curtain to reveal the shenanigans. There is no great and powerful Oz, just a man pushing buttons and flipping switches. They recognize in that moment that they've been duped.

And so have we. We've been duped by Hollywood, social media, and corporate America who tell us that money and power should be our gods, gender is fluid, America is racist, and capitalism is evil. Basically, facts do not matter and truth no longer exists.

The truth is that God created human beings in his image and likeness. He created them "male" and "female." Any attempts to redefine sexuality are dangerous and carry dire consequences. Gender is not a social construct; it's a biological reality. Pretending gender "is fluid" will sabotage healthy relationships and undermine the nuclear family.

In his infinite wisdom, God designed human beings to enjoy and benefit from relationships. No relationships are more important and vital to our health, wealth, and security than those within the family unit. Both adults and children experience great benefits from being part of a family; being separated leaves an individual exposed and vulnerable.

Regardless of the hate that surrounds us, our responsibility—particularly as Christians—to those in our culture who are lost and confused is to love and respect everyone, especially those who disagree with us. There are many ways to show kindness, grace, and compassion and one of the best ways is to forgive. We don't have to accept, however, that "love" means a blanket stamp of approval on every lifestyle. We can choose to love someone without liking their personal choices.

Right now, our nation is in crisis. America was built on the concept of personal freedom—the right to own property, peacefully assemble, worship God, build wealth, protect your family, and pursue happiness. But the very foundation of our society is eroding beneath our feet. Individuals who hate America are trying to suppress our freedoms, destroy our economy, and "fundamentally change" our nation to look more like Cuba or Venezuela—the very countries from which many citizens fled to come to America. If our Democracy falls, there will be nowhere left to go.

We have a systemic problem in our country, but it's not racism. It's poverty. Bad actors in government created systems of poverty in order to suppress entire generations of Americans. Those who created the crisis are claiming they have the solution to the very same problem. These are the same individuals dividing our nation across artificial lines and inflating the COVID-19 infection rates in order to keep us locked down.

The push to "defund the police" isn't about curing racial injustice, it's about creating chaos and seizing control. This movement mocks and silences anyone advocating for law and order. Make no mistake, the call to fundamentally change America is a naked grab for power and nothing more.

But the final verdict is not yet in. God is the author and defender of Justice. No one cares for the oppressed more than the Creator of the universe. True conservatism and the gospel of Jesus Christ are making a come-back in America. The only way to enjoy true freedom in our country is to move back *toward* our Constitution, not away from it. The United States Constitution is the only governing system worldwide which ensures equal justice under the law—for all.

There was a time in America when sincere believers in Jesus Christ could support the Democratic party with a clear conscience. Until around the 1980s, Democrats represented the working class. Both sides of my grandparents were registered Democrats their entire lives. Their families immigrated from Europe to find better opportunity. They were honest, hard-working, and devoutly religious.

However, in the last few decades the political left has abandoned its own people. The party who formerly advocated for the middle class now openly embraces late-term abortion, radical Marxist ideology, and is racing toward the legalization of infanticide (i.e., murder) and even pedophilia as part of the protected LGBTQ community. The California legislature, for example, passed a bill in September 2020 which would end automatic registry for some sex-offenders who commit sexual acts with minors.[212]

The window for plausible deniability for dedicated believers in Jesus who continue to support the Democratic party establishment has officially closed.

In contrast, the Trump Administration has done more in recent years to protect the unborn child, defend religious freedom, create economic opportunity for everyone, end sex-trafficking, preserve law and order, and fight for those truly oppressed by an unfair system created by greedy politicians. President Trump also relocated the US embassy to Jerusalem, a move the past two administrations promised but never delivered.

Christian conservativism is back.

This book is a call for us to look beyond all the smoke and mirrors; to ignore the hysteria which bombards us every day. Like Dorothy, we should "pay no attention to that man behind the curtain." When we have the privilege of looking at this from the other side we'll see how in the final analysis, regardless of lies and deception, God is right and his Word is truth.

In the end, we will recognize that God still reigns over the universe. It's His game, His rules. A time is coming when Truth will be revealed and all evil deeds will be exposed. Until then, we should continue to view our lost and broken world through the lens of love & truth.

Appendix

Tips for Leading Small Group Discussions

Thank you for choosing *Through the Lens of Love & Truth* for your small group discussion. At the end of each chapter you find a short discussion guide which includes questions and Scriptures to look up and consider. These are suggestions to help you facilitate a meaningful discussion. Feel free to add questions or skip any which are uncomfortable for you.

Facilitating discussion is more challenging than one might think. The facilitator is responsible to ensure that all parties are engaged and the conversation is not dominated by one or two individuals. I've included some helpful tips and guidelines for facilitating a discussion below.

As you are preparing, don't hesitate to reach out to me with any questions about the upcoming lesson or from the previous week. My email address is <u>loveandtruthbook@gmail.com</u>. Please allow up to three business days for a response.

Establish Ground Rules For the Group

The ground rules of a group discussion are the guidelines that help to keep the discussion on track and prevent it from deteriorating into an argument.

- Take a couple minutes at the beginning of the first meeting to talk through these ground rules and determine if any other ones should be made.

- Everyone should treat everyone else with respect.

- No arguments directed at people—only at ideas and opinions. Disagreement should be respectful—no ridicule.

- Don't interrupt. Listen to the entirety of others' thoughts. (Listen, rather than just running over your own response in your head.)

- Respect the group's time. Try to keep your comments reasonably short and to the point, so that others have a chance to respond.

- Don't become defensive if someone disagrees with you. Allow alternative opinions to be expressed. Encourage the group to seek the truth rather than simply take sides.

Encourage Productive Behaviors

Model the behavior and attitudes you want group members to employ. This may include:

- respecting all group members equally

- advancing the open process

- demonstrating what it means to be a learner by admitting when you're wrong, or don't know a fact or an answer

- asking questions based on statements of others
- listening carefully
- validating the points others make
- supporting your arguments with fact or logic
- accepting criticism
- thinking critically
- giving up the floor when appropriate
- being inclusive and culturally sensitive

Use encouraging body language and tone of voice as well as words. Lean forward when people are talking. For example, keep your body position open and approachable, smile when appropriate, and attend carefully to everyone.

- Give positive feedback for joining the discussion. Smile, repeat group members' points, and show that you value participation.

- Be aware of people's reactions and feelings and try to respond appropriately. If a group member is hurt by others' comments, seems puzzled or confused, or becomes angry or defensive, it's up to you as the discussion leader to be aware of the situation and find a resolution that is unifying and not divisive. See more tips below on Handling Sensitive Situations.

Encourage Productive Discussion

- Ask open-ended questions. In order to advance the discussion, always use questions that can't be answered with a simple yes or no. Instead, questions should require some thought from group members and should ask for answers that include reasons or analysis.

- The difference between "Do you think so-and-so's decision was right?" and "Why do you think so-and-so's decision was or wasn't right?" is huge. While the first question can be answered with a yes or no, the second requires an analysis supporting the speaker's opinion, as well as discussion of the context and reasons for the decision. (See more tips below.)

- Questions starting with the word "Do" tend to be close-ended, meaning they require only a "yes" or "no" in reply.

- Questions starting with the word "What" or "How" are more likely to be open-ended and generate conversation.

- Try starting a question with "Tell me about…" It is open-ended and encourages input.

- If conversation stalls while reading and discussing the scripture verses, you can ask someone to read the same verse in another translation.

- Don't be afraid of silence. Allow individuals time to process and properly respond to questions. If you rush the discussion because you don't want dead air, you may miss valuable input and discourage some from participating who may need more time to prepare their response.

- Control your own biases. While you should point out factual errors or ideas that are inaccurate and disrespectful of others, an open process demands that you not impose your views on the group and that you keep others from doing the same. Pointing out a bias, including your own, and discussing it helps both you and group members try to be objective.

Be Respectful of Everyone's Time

• Start the group at the designated time and close it at the designated time. Even if people appear to be enjoying the conversation, always give them the option of leaving at the set time without making them feel guilty.

• Don't allow someone to dominate the conversation. (See tips below to discourage this.) It's up to you, the small group leader, to keep everyone engaged in the conversation to the extent they are comfortable.

Tips for Handling Sensitive Situations

If someone is attempting to dominate the conversation, here are some tips:

• Try saying, "That is an interesting point, but there are other points of view that need to be heard as well. I think Alice has been waiting to speak..."

• Sit beside them—not across from them—so that you can avoid eye contact after every question.

• In instances where someone becomes emotional and desires the entire focus of the group, give them a couple minutes to talk and then say, "Let's pray for ___." Once you've prayed, steer the conversation in a different direction.

If someone is hurt by another's comment, consider the following:

- It may be important to point out the offense and discuss how to make arguments without getting personal. If group members are confused, revisiting the comments or points that caused the confusion, or restating them more clearly, may be helpful.

- Be aware of the reactions of individuals. This will make it possible to resolve conflict, or to head off unnecessary emotional situations and misunderstandings.

- Recognize that not all conflict is bad. Relationships are hard work. There is often a process to building relationships and sometimes it involves tension. Your responsibility as a small group leader is to "manage" conflict, not prevent it entirely.

Suggested Small Group Schedules

Below are guidelines to help you structure your small group based on the number of weeks you feel will be most productive for your group.

		SESSION LENGTH			
		6-week	8-week	10-week	12-week
W E E K	#1	1 & 2	1 & 2	1 & 2	1 & 2
	#2	3, 4 & 5	3 & 4	3 & 4	3 & 4
	#3	6 & 7	5 & 6	5 & 6	5
	#4	8, 9 & 10	7 & 8	7 & 8	6
	#5	11 & 12	9	9	7
	#6	13, 14 & CON	10 & 11	10	8
	#7		12 & 13	11	9
	#8		14 & CON	12	10
	#9			13	11
	#10			14 & CON	12
	#11				13
	#12				14 & CON

"CON" = Conclusion

Acknowledgments

The concepts in this book developed over many years, long before they were ever written on paper. I would like to thank the following people for making this vision a reality:

- My husband, Perry, for your insights. This couldn't happen without you.

- Tammy Summers, for all the help you provided on this project by advising, supporting, and co-writing Chapter 14.

- My advisory committee for your guidance: Pastor Mark Lutz, Nick DiRobbio, Ruthann Bowen, Valerie Donnelly, Steve Deal, and Connie Geier.

- Special thanks to Nate Travis for proofreading help.

About the Author

Amy is the founder of FUSION Leadership Group and author of *You Can Visit, But You Can't Live There: Keys to Living Free from Fear, Anxiety, and Guilt.* After high school, she studied theology at Wheaton College for two years but left to marry Perry and start a family. Twenty years later, she completed her bachelor's degree in Psychology at Liberty University. She also obtained a master's degree in Organizational Leadership from South University, as well as several certifications in business, including Project Management Professional (PMP) and Six Sigma. Additionally, Amy holds a ministry license.

This project evolved when Amy recognized the disconnect between the foundational truths found in the Bible and how those principles are applied in a post-postmodern culture where truth is considered subjective and everyone's opinion is regarded as equal.

Amy and Perry have been married for over thirty-two years and have three adult children: Nathan is active-duty US Air Force, Valerie and her husband Cody are police officers, and Nicholas is heading to the Navy after high school.

Contact Amy

Amy can be reached at the email address below for questions or to order multiple books. Discounts are available for bulk orders.

loveandtruthbook@gmail.com

Endnotes

Chapter 1

1   "What Is A World View? - Definition & Introduction," 2019, *Asa3. org*, https://www.asa3.org/ASA/education/views/index.html.

2   "A Biblical Worldview Has A Radical Effect On A Person's Life - Barna Group," 2003, *Barna Group*, https://www.barna.com/research/a-biblical-worldview-has-a-radical-effect-on-a-persons-life/.

3   McCallister, Doreen. 2020. "NPR Choice Page," *Npr.org*, https://www.npr.org/sections/thetwo-way/2018/02/20/587181780/rules-for-2018-aim-to-speed-up-how-long-it-takes-to-play-a-mlb-game.

4   Brothers Osbourne, "It Ain't My Fault, September 2, track 3, *So Good*, TEN Music Group, Epic Records, and Sony Music, 2016.

Chapter 2

5   "Answers In Genesis," 2020, *Answers In Genesis*, https://answersingenesis.org/.

6   "Answers In Genesis," 2020, *Answers In Genesis*, https://answersingenesis.org/.

7   Tanghe, Koen. 2018. "On The Origin Of Species: The Story Of Darwin's Title | Notes And Records: The Royal Society Journal Of The History Of Science," *Royalsocietypublishing.org*, https://royalsocietypublishing.org/doi/10.1098/rsnr.2018.0015.

8   "Definition Of MATERIALISM," 2020, *Merriam-Webster.com*, https://www.merriam-webster.com/dictionary/materialism.

9   Evolutionists, Irreducible, and John Woodmorappe, 2020, "Irreducible Complexity: Some Candid Admissions By Evolutionists," *Answers In Genesis*, https://answersingenesis.org/evidence-against-evolution/irreducible-complexity-some-candid-admissions-by-evolutionists/.

10   Del, Tackett. 2020. "Truth Project - Engage!", *Engage!*, https://www.engage-citizen.com/truth-project/.

11   Purdom, Dr. Georgi. 2020. "Variety Within Created Kinds," *Answers In Genesis*, https://answersingenesis.org/creation-science/baraminology/variety-within-created-kinds/.

12   Howell, Elizabeth. 2020. "What Is The Big Bang Theory?", *Space.com*, https://www.space.com/25126-big-bang-theory.html.

13   "Answers In Genesis," 2020, *Answers In Genesis*, https://answersingenesis.org/.

Chapter 3

14   Romans 3:23

15   Duignan, Brian. 2020. "Gaslighting | Definition, Origins, & Facts," *Encyclopedia Britannica*, https://www.britannica.com/topic/gaslighting.

16   John 3:16

Chapter 4

17   Bucktin, Christopher. 2016. https://www.mirror.co.uk/sport/boxing/muhammad-alis-brother-reveals-knew-8116486.

18   Hebrews 4:15

19   Huda, "Who Wrote the Quran and When?", Learn Religions, https://www.learnreligions.com/compilation-of-the-quran-2004545 (accessed November 14, 2020).

20   "The Dead Sea Scrolls | The Israel Museum, Jerusalem," 2018, *Imj.org.Il*, https://www.imj.org.il/en/wings/shrine-book/dead-sea-scrolls.

21   "What Is Nirvana?", 2020, *Buddhism For Beginners*, https://tricycle.org/beginners/buddhism/what-is-nirvana/.

22   Pastor Chris Marshall, Lead pastor of New Life Christian Ministries.

Chapter 5

23   Symons, Joanna. 2018. "Mothers Asked Nearly 300 Questions A Day, Study Finds," *The Telegraph*, https://www.telegraph.co.uk/news/uknews/9959026/Mothers-asked-nearly-300-questions-a-day-study-finds.html.

24   Kreeft, Peter, Ronald K Tacelli. 2009. *Handbook Of Catholic Apologetics*, San Francisco, Calif.: Ignatius Press.

25   Founder & Teacher, desiringGod.org, 2019, "Are God's Providence And God's Sovereignty The Same? #1383," Podcast, *Ask Pastor God*.

26   Morin, Amy. 2019. "The Critical Difference Between Consequences And Punishments For Kids," *Verywell Family*, https://www.verywellfamily.com/consequences-punishments-differences-kids-1094787.

27   "Gilbert K. Chesterton Quotes," 2018, *Brainyquote*, https://www.brainyquote.com/quotes/gilbert_k_chesterton_156933.

Chapter 6

28   *"Humanae Vitae,"* The Vatican, July 25, 1968.

29   "Full Text: Sister Dede Byrne's Speech At The 2020 Republican National Convention," 2020, *National Catholic Register,* https://www.ncregister.com/daily-news/full-text-sister-dede-byrnes-speech-at-the-2020-republican-national-convent.

30   "Abolishing Abortion: The History Of The Pro-Life Movement In America | The American Historian," 2020, *Oah.org,* https://www.oah.org/tah/issues/2016/november/abolishing-abortion-the-history-of-the-pro-life-movement-in-america/.

31   "Abortion In The United States By State," 2020, *En.Wikipedia.org,* https://en.wikipedia.org/wiki/Abortion_in_the_United_States_by_state.

32   2020, *Plannedparenthood.org.*

33   "NPR Choice Page," 2020, Npr.org, https://www.npr.org/sections/publiceditor/2011/09/19/140612867/abortion-language-politically-correct-or-politically-bomb-throwing#:~:text=In%20an%20attempt%20to%20be,clinic%22%20are%20unfair%2C%20too.

34   Rasha, Ali. 2020. *Usatoday.com,* https://www.usatoday.com/story/life/parenting/2019/09/13/safe-haven-laws-things-you-didnt-know-surrendering-newborn/2031516001/.

35   "The History & Impact Of Planned Parenthood," 2020, *Plannedparenthood.org,* https://www.plannedparenthood.org/about-us/who-we-are/our-history.

36   2020, *History.com,* https://www.history.com/topics/germany/eugenics.

37   "Negro Project," 2020, *Sangervideo.com,* http://www.sangervideo.com/negroproject.html.

38   "The Public Papers Of Margaret Sanger: Web Edition," 2020, *Nyu.edu,* https://www.nyu.edu/projects/sanger/webedition/app/documents/show.php?sangerDoc=306638.xml&_ga=2.28799861.811420770.1598973365-396615015.1598559056.

39   "Negro Project," 2020, *Sangervideo.com,* http://www.sangervideo.com/negroproject.html.

40   "Negro Project," 2020, *Sangervideo.com,* http://www.sangervideo.com/negroproject.html.

41   "Kanye West Proclaims Pro-Life Views," 2020, *Right To Life UK,* https://righttolife.org.uk/news/kanye-west-proclaims-pro-life-views/.

42   "Kanye West Proclaims Pro-Life Views," 2019, *Right To Life UK,* https://righttolife.org.uk/news/kanye-west-proclaims-pro-life-views/.

43   "Klassen: Kanye West Is Changing The Face Of The Pro-Life Movement - Alpha News," 2020, *Alpha News*, https://alphanewsmn. com/klassen-kanye-west-is-changing-the-face-of-the-pro-life-movement/.

44   "Kanye West Proclaims Pro-Life Views," 2019, *Right To Life UK*, https://righttolife.org.uk/news/kanye-west-proclaims-pro-life-views/.

45   Harris, David J. 2018. *Why I Couldn't Stay Silent*, DJHJ Media, LLC.

46   Harris, David J. 2018. *Why I Couldn't Stay Silent*, DJHJ Media, LLC.

47   Ingles, Jo. 2019. "In 2019, Ohio Passed Its Most Restrictive Abortion Law In Modern History," *Radio,Wosu.org*, https://radio.wosu. org/post/2019-ohio-passed-its-most-restrictive-abortion-law-modern-history#stream/0.

Chapter 7

48   Publishing, Harvard, 2019, "Marriage And Men's Health - Harvard Health," *Harvard Health*, https://www.health.harvard.edu/ mens-health/marriage-and-mens-health.

49   Publishing, Harvard, 2019, "Marriage And Men's Health - Harvard Health," *Harvard Health*, https://www.health.harvard.edu/ mens-health/marriage-and-mens-health.

50   "Love And Money: The Surprising Wealth Predictor |", 2019, *Partners4prosperity.com*, https://partners4prosperity.com/love-and-money/.

51   Landas, Luke. 2019. "Does Getting Married Increase Wealth And Income? - Consumerism Commentary," *Consumerism Commentary*, https://www.consumerismcommentary.com/marriage-increase-wealth/.

52   Wandawa, Vicki. 2012. *Newvision.Co.Ug*, https://www.newvision. co.ug/news/1306753/life-orphan-uganda.

53   Parker, Wayne. 2019. "The Troubling Statistics On Fatherless Children In America," *Liveabout*, https://www.liveabout.com/fatherless-children-in-america-statistics-1270392.

54   "Statistics," 2018, *The Fatherless Generation*, https://thefatherlessgeneration.wordpress.com/statistics/.

55   "A Christian Catalyst For Change: Jack Brewer's Story," 2020, *Falkirk Center For Faith & Liberty*, https://www.falkirkcenter.com/2020/04/09/a-christian-catalyst-for-change-jack-brewers-story/.

56   "BOP: First Step Act Overview," 2020, *Bop.gov*, https://www. bop.gov/inmates/fsa/overview.jsp.

57   "A Christian Catalyst For Change: Jack Brewer's Story," 2020, *Falkirk Center For Faith & Liberty*, https://www.falkirkcenter.com/2020/04/09/a-christian-catalyst-for-change-jack-brewers-story/.

58   "The Unauthorized History Of Socialism," 2020, TV programme, Fox News: Bret Baier,

59   Pletcher, Kenneth. 2020. "One-Child Policy | Definition & Facts," *W88top*, http://www.mdc-ds.com/w88top/1794.html.

60   2020, https://blacklivesmatter.com/.

61   Blue Bloods, Season 7, episode 11, 2017.

62   John 8:44

Chapter 8

63   Sopelsa, Brooke. 2020. "Amy Coney Barrett Apologizes For Use Of Phrase 'Sexual Preference,'" *NBC News*, https://www.nbcnews.com/feature/nbc-out/amy-coney-barrett-apologizes-use-phrase-sexual-preference-n1243285.

64   Ibid

65   Murphee, Randall. 2020. "AFA Journal - Pediatrician Champions Truth Versus Transgender Insanity," *AFA Journal*, https://afajournal.org/past-issues/2020/may/pediatrician-champions-truth-versus-transgender-insanity/.

66   "What Is Gender Dysphoria?", 2019, *Psychiatry.org*, https://www.psychiatry.org/patients-families/gender-dysphoria/what-is-gender-dysphoria.

67   Dolphins, Jotaro. 2020. "Complete List Of Genders - The Complete List Of All Genders – Wattpad," *Wattpad.com*, https://www.wattpad.com/341462536-complete-list-of-genders-the-complete-list-of-all.

68   Ibid

69   Desanctis, Alexandra. 2020. "'Sex'- Trump Administration Reverses Obama-Era Regulation That Redefined Term | National Review," *Nationalreview.com*, https://www.nationalreview.com/2020/06/trump-administration-reverses-obama-era-regulation-that-redefined-sex/.

70   Vitale, Ali. 2017. "White House Rolls Back Obama-Era Transgender Bathroom Protections," *NBC News*, https://www.nbcnews.com/politics/white-house/white-house-reverses-obama-era-transgender-bathroom-protections-n724426.

71   Vitale, Ali. 2017. "White House Rolls Back Obama-Era Transgender Bathroom Protections," *NBC News*, https://www.nbcnews.com/politics/white-house/white-house-reverses-obama-era-transgender-bathroom-protections-n724426.

72   Desanctis, Alexandra. 2020. "'Sex'- Trump Administration Reverses Obama-Era Regulation That Redefined Term | National Review," *Nationalreview.com*, https://www.nationalreview.com/2020/06/trump-administration-reverses-obama-era-regulation-that-redefined-sex/.

73   Ellis Nutt, Amy. 2017. https://omaha.com/livewellnebraska/health/johns-hopkins-will-resume-gender-reassignment-surgeries-after--year/article_0c370372-1aee-11e7-8049-d3ae3854aff5.html?utm_medium=social&utm_source=email&utm_campaign=user-share.

74   Ellis Nutt, Amy. 2017. https://omaha.com/livewellnebraska/health/johns-hopkins-will-resume-gender-reassignment-surgeries-after--year/article_0c370372-1aee-11e7-8049-d3ae3854aff5.html?utm_medium=social&utm_source=email&utm_campaign=user-share.

75   Heyer, Walt. 2018. "9 Trans Patients Lodge Shocking Complaints About Sex-Change Surgeries," *The Federalist*, https://thefederalist.com/2018/12/06/9-transgender-patients-complain-mutilation-botched-sex-change-surgeries-oregon/.

76   Segar, Mike. 2020. "Joe Biden Says Young Children Who Decide They 'Want To Be Transgender' Should Face 'Zero Discrimination,'" *RT International*, https://www.rt.com/usa/503659-biden-child-transgenderism-claims/.

77   Ibid

78   Eaton-Robb, Pat. 2019. "Transgender Sprinters Finish 1St, 2Nd At Connecticut Girls Indoor Track Championships," *The Washington Times*, https://www.washingtontimes.com/news/2019/feb/24/terry-miller-andraya-yearwood-transgender-sprinter/.

79   Carlson, Tucker. 2018. "Twitter," *Twitter.com*, https://twitter.com/tuckercarlson/status/948370452656861186?lang=en.

Chapter 9

80   "War Of 1812," 2020, *American Battlefield Trust*, https://www.battlefields.org/learn/war-1812.

81   "Battle Of Fort Mchenry Facts & Summary," 2020, *American Battlefield Trust*, https://www.battlefields.org/learn/war-1812/battles/fort-mchenry.

82   "Battle Of Fort Mchenry Facts & Summary," 2020, *American Battlefield Trust*, https://www.battlefields.org/learn/war-1812/battles/fort-mchenry.

83   Allen, Virginia. 2020. "A List Of America's Toppled, Defaced, Or Removed Statues," *The Daily Signal*, https://www.dailysignal.com/2020/07/17/vandalizing-american-history-a-list-of-64-toppled-defaced-or-removed-statues/.

84   "Sign The Petition," 2019, *Change.org*, https://www.change.org/p/remove-under-god-from-the-u-s-pledge-of-allegiance.

85   Hicks, Allen. 2020. "What Happened After The Declaration Of Independence Was Signed?", *Allanhicks*, https://allanhicks.wordpress.com/2012/07/03/what-happened-after-the-declaration-of-independence-was-signed/.

86   Tolles, Frederick. 2020. "William Penn - Founding And Governorship Of Pennsylvania," *Encyclopedia Britannica*, https://www.britannica.com/biography/William-Penn-English-Quaker-leader-and-colonist/Founding-and-governorship-of-Pennsylvania.

87   "List Of Monuments And Memorials Removed During The George Floyd Protests," 2020, *En.Wikipedia.org*, https://en.wikipedia.org/wiki/List_of_monuments_and_memorials_removed_during_the_George_Floyd_protests.

88   "SHARIA LAW — LIST OF KEY RULES — What Is Sharia Law?", 2019, *Billionbibles.org*, https://www.billionbibles.org/sharia/sharia-law.html.

89   @boissolm, Follow, 2020, "The True Story Of The Reichstag Fire And The Nazi Rise To Power," *Smithsonian Magazine*, https://www.smithsonianmag.com/history/true-story-reichstag-fire-and-nazis-rise-power-180962240/.

90   Ibid

91   Tsarfati, Amir. 2020. Happening Now Jack Hibbs Interview by . In person, Calvary Hills Church, Chino Hills, CA.

Chapter 10

92   "More Poverty Than Ever Before |", 2020, *Therealcuba.com*, https://therealcuba.com/?page_id=273.

93   Fox Nation, Bair, Brett, 2020, *The Unauthorized History Of Socialism*, Video, https://nation.foxnews.com/watch/fe54b3f144aa809b-875c147c037c2fa9/.

94   Smithha, Frank. 2018. "Socialist Experiment In Tanzania: 1961-85," *Fsmitha.com*, http://www.fsmitha.com/h2/ch34-tan.htm.

95   Fox Nation, Bair, Brett, 2020, *The Unauthorized History Of Socialism*, Video.

96   "Top 5 Failed Socialist Promises: From Lenin To Chavez," 2020, *Fox News*, https://www.foxnews.com/politics/top-5-failed-socialist-promises-from-lenin-to-chavez.

97   Cohen, Luc. 2020. "Explainer: Why Oil-Rich Venezuela Is Suffering Severe Gasoline Shortages," *U.S.*, https://www.reuters.com/article/us-venezuela-gasoline-explainer-idUSKBN22V32G.

98   Sequera, Vivian. 2018. "Venezuelans Report Big Weight Losses In 2017 As Hunger Hits," *U.S.*, https://www.reuters.com/article/us-venezuela-food-idUSKCN1G52HA.

99   Margolis, Jason. 2019. "Venezuela Was Once The Richest, Most Stable, Democracy In Latin America. What Happened?", *The World From PRX*, https://www.pri.org/stories/2019-02-07/venezuela-was-once-richest-most-stable-democracy-latin-america-what-happened.

100   https://www.businessinsider.com/alexandria-ocasio-cortez-explains-what-democratic-socialism-means-2019-3?op=1

101   Administration, Veterans, 2020, "VA.gov | Veterans Affairs," *Va. vov*, https://www.va.gov/health/.

102   "'SEAL Team' Exposes VA: 'A Health Care System That Runs Like The Post Office,'" 2019, *Newsbusters*, https://www.newsbusters.org/blogs/culture/lindsay-kornick/2019/04/25/seal-team-exposes-va-health-care-system-runs-post-office.

103   "Barack Obama VA Scandal: 6 Facts About Veterans Health Administration Controversy," Newsmax, Newsmax Media, Inc., 22 Dec. 2014, www.newsmax.com/FastFeatures/barack-obama-scandal-facts/2014/12/22/id/613907/.

104   "Economy Of Sweden," 2020, *En.Wikipedia.org*, https://en.wikipedia.org/wiki/Economy_of_Sweden.

105   Feld, Stanley, 2020, "Swedes Are Frustrated Over Their Socialized Healthcare System," *Repairing The Healthcare System*, https://stanleyfeldmdmace.typepad.com/repairing_the_healthcare_/2020/01/swedes-are-frustrated-over-their-socialized-healthcare-system-.html.

106   Hjertqvist, Johan. 2015. *Thelocal.Se*, https://www.thelocal.se/20150127/swedens-health-care-is-a-shame-to-the-country.

107   Hjertqvist, Johan. 2015. *Thelocal.Se*, https://www.thelocal.se/20150127/swedens-health-care-is-a-shame-to-the-country.

108   Pour, Nima. 2020. "Sweden And Its Welfare State In Crisis," *Gatestone Institute*, https://www.gatestoneinstitute.org/15414/sweden-welfare-crisis.

109   Ibid

110   Hjertqvist, Johan. 2015. *Thelocal.Se*, https://www.thelocal.se/20150127/swedens-health-care-is-a-shame-to-the-country.

111   "Boris Johnson | Biography, Facts, & Role In Brexit," 2020, *Encyclopedia Britannica*. https://www.britannica.com/biography/Boris-Johnson.

112   2020, *History.com*, https://www.history.com/topics/british-history/margaret-thatcher.

113   2 Thessalonians 3:10

114   Kirk, C. 2020. October 11, "Was Jesus a Solialist," [Instagram Post], Phoenix, AZ: Turning Point USA.

115   "Why Socialism Always Results In Tyrannical Rule," 1998, *Orthodoxnet.com*, https://www.orthodoxnet.com/news/WhySocialismAlwaysResultsInTyranny.html.

116   "Friedrich Hayek," 2020, *En.Wikipedia.org*, https://en.wikipedia.org/wiki/Friedrich_Hayek.

Chapter 11

117   "Uzbekistan," 2020, *En.Wikipedia.org*, https://en.wikipedia.org/wiki/Uzbekistan.

118   Griffin, Chris. 2020. Uzbekistan and their Quest for Religious Freedom, Interview by Amy L. Travis, Interview, In person, PIttsburgh, PA.

119   Ibid

120   Fox Nation, Bair, Brett, 2020, *The Unauthorized History Of Socialism*, Video.

121   Silver, Caleb. 2020. "The Top 20 Economies In The World," *Investopedia*, https://www.investopedia.com/insights/worlds-top-economies/#1-united-states.

122   Gye, Hugo. 2020. "America IS The 1%: You Need Just $34,000 Annual Income To Be In The Global Elite... And HALF The World's Richest People Live In The U.S.," *Mail Online*, https://www.dailymail.co.uk/news/article-2082385/We-1--You-need-34k-income-global-elite--half-worlds-richest-live-U-S.html.

123   Albrecht, Leslie. 2020. "The U.S. Is The No. 1 Most Generous Country In The World For The Last Decade," *Marketwatch*, https://www.marketwatch.com/story/the-us-is-the-most-generous-country-but-americans-say-debt-is-keeping-them-from-giving-more-to-charity-2019-10-18.

124   Albrecht, Leslie. 2020. "The U.S. Is The No. 1 Most Generous Country In The World For The Last Decade," *Marketwatch*, https://www.marketwatch.com/story/the-us-is-the-most-generous-country-but-americans-say-debt-is-keeping-them-from-giving-more-to-charity-2019-10-18.

125   Rezaian, Jason. 2020. https://www.washingtonpost.com/opinions/2020/05/28/how-immigrant-ingenuity-is-helping-restaurants-rise-pandemic-challenge/.

126   2020, *Optimistdaily.com*, https://www.optimistdaily.com/2020/04/the-clever-strategies-small-businesses-are-using-to-survive-quarantine/.

127 "Bottled Water History," 2020, *Nestlé Waters US.*, https://www.nestle-watersna.com/who-we-are/our-history/bottledwaterhistory.

128 Mentioff, Rachel. 2019. "Maryland Students' Reading Proficiency Scores Drop In 2019," *Baltimore.Cbslocal.com*, https://baltimore.cbslocal.com/2019/10/30/baltimore-maryland-education-nations-report-card/.

129 Ibid

130 Papst, Chris. 2020. "13 Baltimore City High Schools, Zero Students Proficient In Math," *WBFF*, https://foxbaltimore.com/news/project-baltimore/13-baltimore-city-high-schools-zero-students-proficient-in-math.

131 Durden, Tyler. 2020. "End School To Prison Pipeline' - New Kim Klacik Ad Highlights How Liberals Destroyed Baltimore," *Zero Hedge*, https://www.zerohedge.com/political/end-school-prison-pipeline-new-kim-klacik-ad-highlights-how-liberals-destroyed-baltimore.

132 "Bernie Madoff | Biography, Ponzi Scheme, & Facts," 2020, *Encyclopedia Britannica*, https://www.britannica.com/biography/Bernie-Madoff.

133 Kenton, Will. 2020. "Trickle-Down Theory," *Investopedia*, https://www.investopedia.com/terms/t/trickledowntheory.asp.

134 Talgo, Chris. 2019. "From JFK To Trump: 'A Rising Tide (Of Free-Market Policies) Lifts All Boats,'" *Townhall*, https://townhall.com/columnists/christalgo/2019/07/24/jfk-to-trump-a-rising-tide-of-freemarket-policies-lifts-all-boats-n2550472.

135 "JFK - "A Rising Tide Raises All The Boats" - Phrase Meaning And Origin," 2020, *Phrases.org.Uk*, https://www.phrases.org.uk/bulletin_board/42/messages/1052.html.

Chapter 12

136 "In Portland, Protests And Violence Continue -- 3 Months After They Began," 2020, *PBS Newshour*, https://www.pbs.org/newshour/show/in-portland-protests-and-violence-continue-3-months-after-they-began.

137 2020, *Usatoday.com*, https://www.usatoday.com/story/opinion/2020/07/03/police-black-killings-homicide-rates-race-injustice-column/3235072001/.

138 Volanti, Dr. John. 2020. "PTSD Among Police Officers: Impact On Critical Decision Making," *Cops.Usdoj.gov*, https://cops.usdoj.gov/html/dispatch/05-2018/PTSD.html.

139 2020, *Forbes.com*, https://www.forbes.com/athletes/#193b5f3d55ae.

140 Chapman, Michael. 2020. "FLASHBACK: Morgan Freeman On Ending Racism: 'Stop Talking About It' -- Black History Month Is 'Ridic-

ulous,'" *Cnsnews.com*, https://www.cnsnews.com/blog/michael-w-chapman/flashback-morgan-freeman-ending-racism-stop-talking-about-it-black-history.

141 Maher, Gary. 2020. "Morgan Freeman Drops Truth Bomb On Race Hustlers Leaving CNN Embarrassed & Speechless!", *USA Politics Today*, https://www.usapoliticstoday.org/morgan-freeman-drops-truth-bomb/.

142 "<P>10 Black Celebrities Who Have Said Questionable Things About Racism</P>", 2016, *Essence*, https://www.essence.com/celebrity/black-celebrities-racism-doesnt-exist/#82500.

143 2019, *History.com*, https://www.history.com/topics/early-20th-century-us/jim-crow-laws.

144 Urofsky, Melvin. 2020. "Jim Crow Law | History, Facts, & Examples," *Encyclopedia Britannica*, https://www.britannica.com/event/Jim-Crow-law.

145 2009, *History.com*, https://www.history.com/topics/black-history/plessy-v-ferguson.

146 2020, *History.com*, https://www.history.com/topics/black-history/brown-v-board-of-education-of-topeka.

147 "Browder V. Gayle Filed - African American Registry," 2020, *African American Registry*, https://aaregistry.org/story/browder-v-gayle-filed/.

148 "Oprah Winfrey," 2020, *Biography*, https://www.biography.com/media-figure/oprah-winfrey.

149 "7 Richest Most Powerful Ethnic Groups In America," 2018, *Insider Monkey*, https://www.insidermonkey.com/blog/7-richest-most-powerful-ethnic-groups-in-america-653720/7/.

150 "Economic Opportunity Act Of 1964," 2020, *En.Wikipedia.org*, https://en.wikipedia.org/wiki/Economic_Opportunity_Act_of_1964.

151 "Black America Before LBJ's &Quot;Great Society&Quot;: How The Welfare State Helped Ruin Black Communities," 2020, *Ammo.com*, https://ammo.com/articles/lbj-great-society-war-on-poverty-welfare-state-helped-ruin-black-communities.

152 Delmont, Matthew. 2020. "What Black Americans Lost By Aligning With The Democrats," *The Atlantic*, https://www.theatlantic.com/politics/archive/2016/03/exit-left/476190/.

153 Ibid

154 "Reagan Condemns Welfare System, Says It's Made Poverty Worse Instead Of Better," 2020, *Los Angeles Times*, https://www.latimes.com/archives/la-xpm-1986-02-16-mn-8585-story.html.

155 "African-American Family Structure," 2018, *En.Wikipedia.org*, https://en.wikipedia.org/wiki/African-American_family_structure.

156 "3 Ways The 1994 Crime Bill Continues To Hurt Communities Of Color - Center For American Progress," 2018, *Center For American Progress*, https://www.americanprogress.org/issues/race/news/2019/05/10/469642/3-ways-1994-crime-bill-continues-hurt-communities-color/.

157 School, Stanford, 2020, "Three Strikes Basics | Stanford Law School," *Stanford Law School*, https://law.stanford.edu/stanford-justice-advocacy-project/three-strikes-basics/.

158 Instagram post from Joelpatrick1776, August 28, 2020.

159 Instagram post from Joelpatrick1776, October 15, 2020.

160 Instagram post from Dineshjdsouza, August 9, 2020.

161 "America The Least Racist Country - Www.Elizabethton.com," 2020, https://www.elizabethton.com/2020/06/09/america-the-least-racist-country/.

Chapter 13

162 Cunningham, William. 2020. "Black Lives Matter: Corporate America Has Pledged $1.678 Billion So Far," *Black Enterprise*, https://www.blackenterprise.com/black-lives-matter-corporate-america-has-pledged-1-678-billion-so-far/.

163 Pavlich, Katie. 2020. "Cost Of Recent Riot Damages Are The Worst In U.S. History," *Townhall*, https://townhall.com/tipsheet/katiepavlich/2020/09/16/the-financial-cost-of-recent-riots-has-been-tabulated-n2576294.

164 Ibid

165 "Social Justice Definition," 2020, *Investopedia*. https://www.investopedia.com/terms/s/social-justice.asp.

166 2020, https://www.wtsp.com/article/features/defund-the-police-origin/67-9271557c-89e0-48ab-8e45-fa0dd1ae9c09.

167 Ibid

168 Ibid

169 GRZESZCZAK, JOCELYN. 2020. "81% Of Black Americans Don't Want Less Police Presence Despite Protests—Some Want More Cops: Poll," *Newsweek*, https://www.newsweek.com/81-black-americans-dont-want-less-police-presence-despite-protestssome-want-more-cops-poll-1523093.

170 "Memphis, TN Crime Rates And Statistics – Neighborhood scout," 2020, *Neighborhoodscout.com*, https://www.neighborhoodscout.com/tn/memphis/crime#data.

171   McCarthy, Niall. 2020. "Major American Cities See Sharp Spike In Murders In 2020 [Infographic]," *Forbes*, https://www.forbes.com/sites/niallmccarthy/2020/08/04/major-american-cities-see-sharp-spike-in-murders-in-2020-infographic/?sh=33f94b5b5af2.

172   McCarthy, Niall. 2020. "Major American Cities See Sharp Spike In Murders In 2020 [Infographic]," *Forbes*, https://www.forbes.com/sites/niallmccarthy/2020/08/04/major-american-cities-see-sharp-spike-in-murders-in-2020-infographic/?sh=33f94b5b5af2.

173   Hart, Kim. 2020. "The Cities That Are Already Defunding The Police," *Axios*, https://www.axios.com/cities-defund-the-police-george-floyd-188e169a-a32a-44fa-bace-e2e5df4d1c9b.html.

174   Graves, Lucia. 2011. "Huffpost Is Now A Part Of Verizon Media," *Huffpost.com*, https://www.huffpost.com/entry/crack-powder-sentencing-d_n_667317.

175   Ibid

176   "Alice Marie Johnson," 2020, *En.Wikipedia.org*, https://en.wikipedia.org/wiki/Alice_Marie_Johnson.

177   "BOP: First Step Act Overview," 2020, *Bop.gov*, https://www.bop.gov/inmates/fsa/overview.jsp.

178   Ibid

179   Ibid

180   Elliot, Chris. 2020. "Civil Rights Attorney, Lifelong Democrat: President Trump Has Done More For Blacks Than Obama," *Law Enforcement Today*, https://www.lawenforcementtoday.com/civil-rights-attorney-trump-has-done-more-for-blacks-than-obama/.

181   Johnson, Jeremiah. 2020. "Jeremiah Johnson Ministries On Facebook Watch," *Facebook Watch*, https://www.facebook.com/watch/live/?v=638558523748627&ref=watch_permalink.

182   "A Biblical Worldview Has A Radical Effect On A Person's Life - Barna Group," 2003, *Barna Group*.

183   Matthew 10:16

184   Judges 17:6

185   September 19, 2020

186   Brody, David. 2020. "'I Believe God Put Me In This Place For A Purpose': New WH Press Secretary On Faith, Love Of Country, And Overcoming Adversity," *CBN News*, https://www1.cbn.com/cbn-news/us/2020/may/i-believe-god-put-me-in-this-place-for-a-purpose-new-wh-press-secretary-on-faith-love-of-country-and-overcoming-adversity.

187   Instagram @AbbyJohnson on 11/12/20.

188 "Coronavirus Outbreak: The Countries Affected So Far," 2020, *Clinicaltrialsarena.com*, https://www.clinicaltrialsarena.com/features/coronavirus-outbreak-the-countries-affected/.

189 "Karli Bone," 2020, *Instagram.com*, https://www.instagram.com/tv/CEHw75jH8qS/?igshid=8rt9ulb3u87o&fbclid=IwAR3QRT-1SubvX_FFTSzCYR0QJc0kJwh4B4h_KctG281J8CyRv7iQEfZKP90U.

190 2017, "8 Hurricanes That Struck The US In 2017," *Worldatlas*, https://www.worldatlas.com/articles/8-hurricanes-that-struck-the-us-in-2017.html.

191 "Global Volcanism Program | Current Eruptions," 2020, *Smithsonian Institution | Global Volcanism Program*, https://volcano.si.edu/gvp_currenteruptions.cfm.

192 "America'S Drug Overdose Epidemic: Data To Action," 2019, *Centers For Disease Control And Prevention*, https://www.cdc.gov/injury/features/prescription-drug-overdose/index.html.

Chapter 14

193 Writer, Staff, 2020, "How Large Is Israel?", *Reference.com*, https://www.reference.com/geography/large-israel-67caca9bcf-7f65ae.

194 "Largest Natural Gas Reserve Discovered In Israel Worth Approximately $95 Billion," 2010, *Haaretz.com*, https://www.haaretz.com/largest-natural-gas-reserve-discovered-in-israel-worth-approximately-1.5100884.

195 2017, *Abouthungary.Hu*, http://abouthungary.hu/news-in-brief/israels-prime-minister-benjamin-netanyahu-meets-v4-heads-of-state/.

196 "Benjamin Netanyahu Begins East Africa Trip In Uganda," 2016, *Aljazeera.com*, https://www.aljazeera.com/news/2016/7/4/benjamin-netanyahu-begins-east-africa-trip-in-uganda.

197 "Russian Gas Pipeline To Germany Sows Divisions In Europe And Beyond," 2019, *Los Angeles Times*, https://www.latimes.com/world/la-fg-russia-nordstream2-gas-pipeline-20190625-story.html.

198 Ibid

199 "Cyrus The Great | Biography & Facts," 2020, *Encyclopedia Britannica*, https://www.britannica.com/biography/Cyrus-the-Great.

200 "Nuclear Deal: Is Iran's Economy Better Off Now?", 2018, *BBC News*, https://www.bbc.com/news/world-middle-east-43975498.

201 "Trump Administration Is Pulling The US Out Of UN Human Rights Council, Report Says," 2018, *The Independent*, https://www.independent.co.uk/news/world/americas/us-politics/trump-us-un-human-rights-council-nikki-haley-israel-north-korea-iran-a8401281.html.

202 Davidson, Jordan. 2020. "Trump Secures Third Historic Middle East Peace Deal, This Time With Sudan," *The Federalist*, https://thefederalist.com/2020/10/23/trump-secures-third-historic-middle-east-peace-deal-this-time-with-sudan/.

203 "Ezekiel's War," 2020, *Versebyverseministry.org*, https://www.versebyverseministry.org/bible-answers/when-does-the-war-of-ezekiel-38-39-take-place.

204 "Obama's Egyptian Blunder | Realclearpolitics," 2016, *Realclearpolitics.com*, https://www.realclearpolitics.com/articles/2016/01/29/obamas_egyptian_blunder_129477.html#!.

205 "180,000 Killed, 6 Million Displaced In Arab Spring," 2013, *World Bulletin / News From Turkey And Islamic World*, https://www.world-bulletin.net/middle-east/180000-killed-6-million-displaced-in-arab-spring-h125344.html.

206 "The Arab Uprisings In 2020: There Is No Return To The Old Status Quo," 2020, *Middle East Eye*, https://www.middleeasteye.net/opinion/what-will-2020-bring-middle-east-and-north-africa.

207 Ibid

208 Johnson, Brad. 2020. "Erdogan Puts Israel Next In List For Conquest," *Americans For Intelligence Reform*, https://intelreform.org/2020/07/31/erdogans-dangerous-activities-escalating-towards-war/.

209 "Ottoman Empire | Facts, History, & Map," 2020, *Encyclopedia Britannica*, https://www.britannica.com/place/Ottoman-Empire.

210 Johnson, Brad. 2020. "Erdogan Puts Israel Next In List For Conquest," *Americans For Intelligence Reform*, https://intelreform.org/2020/07/31/erdogans-dangerous-activities-escalating-towards-war/.

211 Matthew 16:3

Conclusion

212 Margolis, Matt. 2020. "CA Legislature Passes Bill Easing Punishment For Pedophiles Because Of 'LGBTQ Equality' Or Something," *Pjmedia.com*, https://pjmedia.com/news-and-politics/matt-margolis/2020/09/03/ca-legislature-passes-bill-easing-punishment-for-pedophiles-because-of-lgbtq-equality-or-something-n885940.